Nonprofit, Inc

Nonprofit, Inc: Scaling with Purpose bridges the persistent gap between theory and practice in the nonprofit sector. Drawing on decades of strategic advisory experience and real-world data, author Carol Wick introduces her Five Factors™ Framework: a practical model used to assess and strengthen organizational capacity across five essential areas: plan, outcomes, budget, team, and funding.

Rooted in systems thinking, human-centered leadership, and applied strategy, this book offers a new approach to sustainable nonprofit growth. Wick combines diagnostic tools, case studies, and actionable guidance to help leaders align mission with operations, replace survival mode with strategic clarity, and scale what works, all without losing their soul in the process.

Designed for nonprofit executives, board members, funders, consultants, and graduate programs in nonprofit management and philanthropy, *Nonprofit, Inc* is both a conceptual framework and an implementation guide. Readers will walk away with the tools to lead with integrity, the insight to make smarter decisions, and the clarity to grow lasting, measurable impact.

Carol Wick is a mission-driven growth expert, founder of Sharity, and creator of the Five Factors™ Framework. As an award-winning CEO, she has helped raise over $250 million, guided hundreds of organizations to scale with integrity, launched a national nonprofit for survivors, and continues to transform the social sector with bold, equity-centered strategy.

"*Nonprofit, Inc: Scaling With Purpose* is a powerful, uplifting guide for mission-driven leaders. Both inspiring and practical, it offers a clear, step-by-step path for building strong, sustainable, purposeful organizations. This is the book I wish I had had when I began my nonprofit leadership journey; clear, wise, and full of possibility."

Anne Miskey, *National Expert on Homelessness; Former CEO, Funders Together to End Homelessness and Union Station Homeless Services*

"*Nonprofit, Inc: Scaling with Purpose* is an essential resource for emerging and established nonprofits. Carol Wick shows how to align core values with sound business practices and offers a practical framework for strategic decisions. I highly recommend this book to nonprofit professionals, boards, consultants, and nonprofit management students everywhere today."

Cynthia Wood, *Strategic Development and Organizational Consultant, Philanthropy Partner, LLC*

"I've watched visionary nonprofit leaders shrink their ambitions to fit broken systems. This book offers the opposite: a framework strong enough to support the scale, complexity, and heart of the work. These Five Factors™ don't just guide strategy. They unlock real, measurable, lasting impact where it matters most."

Jamie Pulliam, *Nonprofit and Corporate Board Director*

"Having a noble intent and a generous spirit is not enough for charitable organizations to survive. Drawing on decades of practical experience, Carol Wick offers a roadmap to financial health and longevity for nonprofits. *Nonprofit, Inc* is an essential guide for current and future leaders in fundraising and social impact.

Saso Venovski, *Board Member, Rotary Foundation, and Professor of Sociology, Valencia College*

Nonprofit, Inc

Scaling with Purpose

Carol Wick

Routledge
Taylor & Francis Group
NEW YORK AND LONDON

Designed cover image: © Sharity

First published 2026
by Routledge
605 Third Avenue, New York, NY 10158

and by Routledge
4 Park Square, Milton Park, Abingdon, Oxon, OX14 4RN

Routledge is an imprint of the Taylor & Francis Group, an informa business

ISBN: 978-1-041-25332-7 (hbk)
ISBN: 978-1-041-25331-0 (pbk)
ISBN: 978-1-003-74621-8 (ebk)

DOI: 10.4324/9781003746218

Typeset in Optima
by codeMantra

To the nonprofit leaders who never stop trying—
choosing to plan, measure, and lead not for ego,
but for impact.

You are proof that purpose can be powerful.

Contents

Foreword

The nonprofit sector is full of people with big hearts and bold visions. People who step up when others turn away, determined to make the world better. Yet too often, those same people find themselves exhausted, underfunded, and fighting burnout. They juggle crises, chase grants, and struggle to keep the lights on, wondering why making a difference feels so hard.

It's not because they don't care or aren't working hard enough. It's because the system they're working within was never built to help them thrive.

I remember signing up for my first fundraising class decades ago, eager to learn the "secrets" to closing that dreaded gap in the budget. Not long after, I landed my first grant, then another and another. I thought I was on my way. But before long, my life became a loop: build the budget in May, get it approved in June, start chasing the gap in July, and repeat. It felt like *Groundhog Day* for nonprofits. I couldn't shake the question: Why are we all working so hard to stay stuck in the same cycle?

So, I went looking for answers. I realized quickly that what I needed most—real business strategy, finance, and marketing—wasn't being taught at nonprofit conferences. What I found instead were endless sessions on donor cultivation and event planning, but nothing on valuation, sustainability, or how to actually grow an organization. So I went where those lessons were taught: business school.

I'll never forget that first day. A nonprofit workshop was being held in the same building. Paper signs taped to the wall pointed the way to the basement. Upstairs, the business students were greeted at the door and ushered into rooms lined with technology and leather chairs. I felt out of place sitting among executives in suits, but I also knew I was exactly where I needed to be.

There, I learned a different language. I learned how to read financial statements like a map. I learned about product valuation, contract negotiation, and competition—concepts that were almost never discussed in the nonprofit world. I began to understand why some organizations, no matter how noble their mission, could never seem to grow. We were never taught to think like builders. We were taught to survive, not to scale.

Over the years, as I moved into consulting, I realized this was why so many of my clients struggled. Nonprofit leaders have not been taught the right skills to succeed. Our field has been treated as something separate from business, as if heart and strategy can't coexist. But they can. And they must. The truth is, nonprofits and for-profits share the same basic DNA. Both need a clear purpose, sustainable revenue, strong leadership, and a clear way to communicate value to those who invest in them, whether those investors are shareholders or donors.

Where the two differ is not in structure, but in intent. Businesses measure profit; nonprofits measure impact. Both are measures of value. Both rely on trust, clarity, and accountability. And both rise or fall based on how well they can align people around a common purpose.

This book grew out of that realization. For years, I've worked with organizations that care deeply about their missions but struggle to build the systems that make them sustainable. I've seen brilliant leaders burn out, programs close, and opportunities slip away, not because the work wasn't needed, but because the framework around it was broken.

It's time to change that.

My goal in writing this book is simple: to bridge the gap between the heart of the nonprofit world and the discipline of the business world. To show that when we apply the same rigor and strategy used by successful companies, without losing our purpose, we can build organizations that not only survive but thrive.

Because passion can start a movement, but only strategy can sustain one.

Acknowledgments

This book would not exist without the extraordinary people who have shaped, supported, and inspired me along the way.

To my **family**, who have been my constant source of strength, patience, and grounding—thank you for believing in this work and in me through every late night and new idea.

To my **mentors**, whose wisdom and encouragement have guided my thinking and kept me stretching toward new possibilities—your lessons are woven through every page.

And to the **Sharity team**, past and present—thank you for bringing our shared mission to life with creativity, dedication, and courage. You have proven that strategic thinking and heart can coexist, and that purpose, when aligned with action, can truly scale.

This book is as much yours as it is mine.

Introduction—Discovery of the Five Factor™ Framework

Every nonprofit leader grapples with a fundamental question: why do some organizations thrive under pressure while others falter? I've long believed the answer extends beyond charisma, luck, or even mission. My experience leading family violence organizations through challenging times and advising countless nonprofits revealed consistent patterns. The organizations that flourished seemed to possess a quiet order: structural elements that provided stability amidst change.

To test this assumption, my team and I conducted a self-funded study of domestic violence shelters across the Americas. Our goal was to identify what truly defines organizational stability and sustainability, grounded in data, not assumption.

We began by examining what financial advisors teach their high-net-worth clients about philanthropy, specifically, which indicators they use to assess a nonprofit's strength, accountability, and impact.

Using those criteria as our guide, we developed a set of questions to evaluate which organizations demonstrated these elements, which did not, and how that difference affected their long-term sustainability and growth. We assessed five core areas: financial reserves, strategic planning, team capacity, outcomes tracking, and donor engagement.

The results were striking. The few organizations that thrived under pressure consistently showed strength across all five areas. These became what I now call the Five Factors™ Framework.

What we discovered became a roadmap for how nonprofits can move from survival to sustainability.

The consistency of these findings prompted us to expand our research, applying the same analysis to hundreds of nonprofits of all sizes and missions. The pattern held: the presence, or absence, of these five elements predicted not only survival during a crisis but also the ability to scale impact. What began as a single study has evolved into an ongoing international assessment, now used to benchmark nonprofit readiness, resilience, and return on investment.

DOI: 10.4324/9781003746218-1

This book represents the culmination of that journey. It is not a collection of theories but a tested model born from real-world data and refined through years of application. The Five Factors™—**Plan, Outcomes, Budget, Team, and Donors**—offer a roadmap for any organization aiming to grow with purpose, communicate its impact confidently, and attract the transformative investments that make all the difference.

- **Plan**—Do you have a clear plan describing your work and needs?
- **Outcomes**—Do you know your work moves the needle? Do you consistently measure success?
- **Budget**—Do you have a budget that covers the full cost of implementing the plan?
- **Team**—Can your team, including staff, board, and volunteers, implement the plan and raise the necessary funds?
- **Donors**—Do you have donors already cultivated who can fund your work, or will you need to find and cultivate new ones?

From Crisis to Capacity

When you're underfunded, understaffed, and operating in constant crisis mode, it's nearly impossible to step back and plan. Most nonprofit leaders are deeply mission-driven. They care profoundly and work tirelessly, but without time and structure to build internal systems, even the most passionate organizations struggle to demonstrate their effectiveness.

And when they do try, the support they receive is often fragmented. Training typically focuses on one piece: strategic planning, budgeting, or evaluation, without connecting the dots between them. What leaders truly need is a comprehensive, holistic framework that shows how every part of the organization works together to create measurable, investable impact.

That's what this book provides. It's both a training guide and a transformation tool designed to help you grow your nonprofit sustainably by aligning every element of your organization with the expectations of today's philanthropic investors. It outlines what donors look for, explains how those elements interconnect, and offers a blueprint for moving your organization from where you are to where you aspire to be.

This book is for people leading nonprofits of all shapes and sizes. Whether you're just getting started or refining a well-established organization, you'll learn how to strengthen each of the Five Factors™. The framework draws from years of research and real-world experience across hundreds of organizations. What makes it unique is that it bridges two worlds: the nonprofit's drive to serve and the donor's desire to see a return on impact.

Throughout this book, you'll see the term *investor* used instead of *donor*. We explore this distinction in depth later, but for now, think of donors as investors as those who carefully research before making a transformative gift. They're looking for evidence of the Five Factors™—proof that your organization has a sound plan, a capable team, and measurable outcomes that justify significant investment.

Reframing donors as investors changes everything. It shifts the relationship from gratitude to partnership, from "thank you for giving" to "let's build this future together." Investors see their contribution as a long-term commitment to solving a problem. When we adopt that mindset, we create shared accountability, mutual respect, and deeper collaboration. It changes how nonprofits communicate, plan, and deliver results, and how funders perceive value and engage with your work.

The goal is simple: to build organizations that not only do good work but prove they are the best at what they do.

Many nonprofits fall into familiar traps: weak planning, unclear budgets, overstretched staff, and disengaged boards. Rather than look at these as failures, consider them opportunities. Obvious issues are typically easier to diagnose and fix. By strengthening the five foundational factors, you build an organization that inspires confidence, attracts investment, and delivers measurable, lasting change.

You may find that this book raises some uncomfortable questions. That's intentional. Growth begins with honest reflection. Every question is designed to move you closer to clarity, sustainability, and impact for your team, your community, and the cause you serve.

Let's begin by taking an honest look at where your organization stands today.

Five Factors™ Assessment: Measuring Organizational Readiness

This assessment is your compass throughout this book. At the end of each chapter, you'll return to it, scoring your organization across the Five Factors™ to track progress and pinpoint areas that need deeper focus.

To help you identify where your organization is strong and where it may need more focus, the following assessment will guide you through five critical factors that determine organizational health and sustainability: Plan, Outcomes, Budget, Team, and Donors. Together, these areas form the foundation of any successful nonprofit.

The assessment will help you determine whether your organization has a clear and actionable plan, can demonstrate measurable results, has a budget that fully supports its goals, possesses the right mix of people to execute the work, and maintains the donor relationships necessary for long-term stability. By pinpointing your organization's strengths and weaknesses, you can more effectively target improvements and take strategic steps toward greater impact and financial resilience.

Five Factor Nonprofit Readiness Assessment Tool

For each factor, rate your organization again on a scale of **1 to 5**, where **1** means your organization is just beginning or lacks this component, and **5** means your organization is fully operational and consistent in this practice.

Add up the scores across the Five Factors™ for a maximum of **25 points**. A total score of **20 or higher** signals a strong foundation and readiness to attract major support, while anything below that highlights areas that still need development.

I PLAN – Clarity, Strategy, and Alignment

_____ Our mission and vision clearly describe the change we seek to make in the community we serve.

_____ We have a current written strategic plan that identifies our top measurable priorities for the next three to five years.

_____ Our goals and strategies are regularly reviewed, tracked, and updated as conditions change.

_____ Staff, board, and volunteers all understand how their work connects to the organization's goals.

_____ We have clear written processes and policies that ensure consistency across programs and operations.

_____ Decisions are guided by data, alignment with mission, and long-term sustainability, not just urgency.

Average score for this section _____

II OUTCOMES—Measuring Impact and Learning

_____ We define success in terms of measurable outcomes, not just activities or outputs.

_____ We consistently collect and analyze data to understand who we serve and what difference our programs make.

_____ We use client, partner, and community feedback to improve our programs and services.

_____ Our impact stories and data are shared with stakeholders in clear, compelling ways.

_____ We regularly evaluate what is working, discontinue or adjust what isn't, and celebrate progress.

Average score for this section _____

III BUDGET – Financial Strength and Sustainability

_____ We have an accurate, realistic budget aligned with our goals and mission priorities that covers the cost to execute on our three- to five-year plan.

_____ Financial reports are reviewed regularly by leadership and the board to monitor progress and make adjustments.

_____ We understand the true cost of delivering each program or service and use that data for decision-making.

_____ We have diverse and reliable revenue streams that reduce dependence on any one funder.

_____ We can clearly communicate our financial story—including both needs and impact—to donors and funders.

Average score for this section _____

IV TEAM – People, Leadership, and Culture

_____ Our organizational chart and job descriptions are clear, current, and aligned with our mission.

_____ We have the right people in the right roles, with clear performance expectations.

_____ Leadership promotes trust, accountability, and open communication across all levels.

_____ Staff receive regular coaching, recognition, and opportunities for professional growth.

_____ The board is engaged, understands its governance role, and contributes time, expertise, and financial support.

_____ Our values are visible in how we hire, manage, and collaborate—because they guide our culture daily.

Average score for this section _____

V DONORS – Engagement, Communication, and Stewardship

_____We have a written fund development strategy that includes cultivation, solicitation, and stewardship steps for annual and major donors.

_____ We actively identify and build relationships with new potential donors and partners.

_____ We maintain ongoing, personalized communication with current donors to keep them informed and inspired.

_____ Our marketing and fundraising messages clearly explain why our organization is unique and worth investing in.

_____ We track donor interactions and measure fundraising effectiveness to strengthen future outreach.

_____ Donors, funders, and community partners see us as transparent, results-driven, and aligned with their values.

Average score for this section _____

Scoring Guide

Add up your total for each section and divide by the number of questions in that section.

Average	*Meaning*	*Interpretation*
1.0–2.0	Needs attention	Systems or clarity missing; urgent improvement needed.
2.1–3.0	Developing	Some structure in place; inconsistent application or accountability.
3.1–4.0	Effective	Functioning well overall with room for refinement.
4.1–5.0	Strong	Strategic, data-driven, and sustainable—best-practice level.

As you progress through this book, you'll deepen your understanding of what it takes to build a strong, investable organization. This exercise isn't about perfection—it's about progress. Use the Five Factors™ Readiness

Assessment from this introduction as your guidepost. Revisit your original scores and adjust them as your understanding evolves.

Each chapter focuses on one of the Five Factors™—**Plan, Outcomes, Budget, Team, and Donors**—so as you move through the material, you may recognize that what once seemed "good enough" now has room for improvement, or that your earlier assumptions have shifted as your vision becomes clearer.

Chapter 1

Building Your Plan

When I start working with a client, I ask them to tell me their founder's story. I love hearing about the challenge they or someone they cared about faced and how they were driven to address that need. That's how most non-profits emerge and is at the heart of their "why" they exist.

They are launched from a place of pain, passion, and the desire to fill an assumed urgent need rather than from a place of careful planning. Someone sees a problem, steps in to help, and rallies friends and family to support the cause. Rarely do its leaders pause to test assumptions or analyze whether others already address this same need and if their plan is sound. This oversight can create duplication and fragmentation across the nonprofit landscape. Passion alone, while powerful, is not a substitute for strategy.

70% of nonprofits operate without a viable plan.[1]

A plan is the most important tool your nonprofit can have. Done correctly, your plan drives every element of your work, governance, finance, operations, and fundraising. A plan is critical to successful growth. We all know that no successful business hoping to make a profit would launch a new service or product without a detailed strategy. Before a single dollar is asked of investors, questions would have to be answered: Is there real demand for this product? Will customers pay for it at a price that allows a profit? Can the company deliver it more effectively and efficiently than others? Most nonprofits skip this step, and assume the mission alone justifies their work. They rarely pause to ask whether clients need the service, want it in the form or way it is provided, or whether others already do it better. Imagine a startup pitching investors without addressing those questions. It would fail instantly. Yet, nonprofits mistakenly believe they should be held to less rigorous standards, which leaves them vulnerable to inefficiency and donor doubt.

DOI: 10.4324/9781003746218-2

Why Planning Matters

The result of operating without a true plan is predictable: staff burnout, stagnant growth, and declining donor confidence. Teams work hard but struggle to see impact. Boards lose clarity about direction and hesitate to open doors or make introductions. When crises arise, like economic downturns, pandemics, or sudden expenses, organizations without strong plans are often the first to collapse. Major donors gravitate to organizations that are confident and show growth and measurable progress, not those that seem to be standing still, or even worse, struggling.

When nonprofit leaders are asked if they have a plan, most think of a traditional strategic plan that lists priorities for the next few years: improve fundraising, recruit new board members, and enhance visibility. While important, such lists are inward-facing and rarely tied to measurable outcomes or donor engagement. A more effective approach is to treat strategic planning as the nonprofit equivalent of a business plan: a detailed, evidence-based case that proves to funders and stakeholders why the organization exists, what needs it meets, and how it will sustain that work.

A true strategic plan is not a checklist. Rather, it is a roadmap defining where the organization is going, how it will get there, and why it matters. Strong plans connect long-term vision with short-term execution, breaking big goals into clear, time-bound milestones. When planning becomes a living process guiding daily decisions rather than a static document, ambition turns into action.

Donors as Investors

Just as entrepreneurs seek investors, nonprofits must approach donors as partners investing in measurable impact. Major donors view philanthropy through a business lens: they want proof that their contribution produces tangible change. Today's nonprofits must treat planning like a business plan, develop a pitch deck and be practical, data-driven, and donor-ready. Major donors expect the same clarity and accountability they would find in for-profit investments. They want to see a clear need, a credible strategy, and measurable results.[2] The mission alone is no longer enough. It must also be a smart investment.

High-value donors give significant gifts only to organizations that demonstrate planning, outcomes, and the capacity to use funds effectively. Consider MacKenzie Scott's foundation Yield Giving, which has awarded over $19 billion to more than 2,000 nonprofits since 2019. Her team vets organizations rigorously, rewarding those with strong leadership, clear plans, measurable outcomes, and scalable models. Friends of the Children, for example, leveraged a $44 million Scott gift to expand into at least ten more locations, attracting follow-on funding from other major philanthropists.[3] Friends of the Children's success was no accident. It reflected strategic clarity and demonstrated impact.

A robust strategic plan is thus not just an internal management tool but also a signal to investors that the organization knows its market, understands its value, and can deliver results. Due diligence is exhaustive and focuses on five key factors: a clear plan, measurable outcomes, an accurate budget, a reliable team, and engaged donors.

Strong plans share several traits. They are inclusive, realistic, and flexible. They involve every stakeholder, from clients and frontline staff to board members and funders, so that everyone has ownership of the mission and its outcomes. Furthermore, they are designed to adapt to changes in the external environment, acknowledging that the social and economic context can shift quickly. Additionally, they are grounded in measurable, attainable goals rather than lofty statements disconnected from operational capacity.

Organizations with robust plans tend to play offense, not defense. They innovate, take calculated risks, and adjust rapidly when conditions change. Those without plans react instead of lead. Planning forces a nonprofit to confront its realities: What do we do well? Where are we struggling? What resources do we lack? What external factors could threaten or accelerate our mission? The process itself builds resilience.

A well-crafted plan shows that a nonprofit has thought beyond daily operations to the bigger picture. It communicates the foundation for sustainable funding and transformative gifts: confidence, competence, and credibility. Strategic planning, in short, is not a bureaucratic exercise; it's the blueprint that turns purpose into progress and vision into investment.

Building the Framework

Before creating a plan, leaders must ensure they have the time, resources, and commitment to complete the process. Strategic planning requires discipline.

Use these questions to help you set up the foundation of this process.

Who Should Lead the Planning Process?

The first step is establishing a planning committee or team responsible for driving the effort. The key is to involve people who are invested, thoughtful, and willing to see the process through. We often recommend this be a group of no more than five to ten board members, leadership staff, and volunteers.

A planning committee can reduce the amount of time you require from those whose time is limited. For smaller organizations, this group is typically the senior staff and board executive committee. For larger organizations, it might be a larger set of managers and an ad-hoc group of board members who dedicate their time to the planning process. When thinking of whom to engage, consider their past engagement levels, commitment, and level of genuine interest in the organization. Are these individuals likely to see the process? Will they bring motivation or excitement to the project?

What Stakeholders Will We Engage?

Once the team has been assembled, you need to determine who you will engage and what voices need to be heard. Each group brings different insights into strengths, weaknesses, and opportunities. Plan early for how to engage them, through surveys, focus groups, interviews, or community meetings. A realistic timeline is also critical. Rushing the process undermines the very reflection that makes planning valuable.

From clients to partners to staff to board members, it is important to consider the voices of those whose input you need as part of the process. Create a list of stakeholders and a strategy to best engage them. A stakeholder is anyone who has an interest in the organization. This will vary from organization to organization, but this includes staff members, volunteers, clients, people living in the region where services are rendered, donors, and members of the board of directors.

Depending on the organization's focus and the population it serves, the way engagement takes place will differ. For environmentalist groups, perhaps engagement will be stronger with community-wide meetings to discuss a local park initiative, whereas organizations working with the unhoused might find one-on-one meetings with clients a more useful approach. Conditional to the stakeholder and the organization, this will likely involve a variety of approaches, such as surveys, focus groups, one-on-one interviews, and possibly community or street outreach. What is the best way to truly reach all stakeholders?

As part of the engagement process, it is critical to engage those you are working to impact. Too often, well-intentioned nonprofit leaders design solutions in the absence of impacted communities. Top-down approaches like these are not as effective as they could be and can alienate impacted communities and other key stakeholders.

Reaching out to communities the non-profit hopes to affect can help lead to high impact, innovative solutions.

What Is Our Timeline?

A strong plan takes time. You won't develop the plan you need in a weekend or even in a month. Consider the time it will take to gain stakeholder buy-in, refine the plan and goals, and develop metrics and action plans. A typical planning process will take six months to a year. Given the amount of time and dedication to this process, it is crucial you build a strong planning process leadership team that is willing to stick out this lengthy, complex process.

How Much Will This Cost?

Organizations must budget for this effort. Planning should be seen as a critical investment, as it sets the direction for years to come. There are various costs associated with developing a strategic plan. Consider the costs associated with doing interviews, setting up and executing surveys, putting together community meetings, and doing extensive street outreach. This includes the cost of time and resources of both the facilitator and the participant. Consider if you will be compensating those who might have to take time off work to participate. Other costs can include specialty software for statistical analysis and/or transcription during interviews. Once all the information is collected, there are also resources that go into analyzing all the information and using it to develop a strong strategic plan.

For some organizations, the costs associated with some specialty processes, or the learning curve of taking on such work, might be daunting or too resource intensive to take on. In this case, determine if you will engage a facilitator or expert to help guide you through the process. Rather than simply going with a friend of a friend or a board member, consider issuing a request for proposals and seeing who could lead this process for you. There is tremendous talent in this space, led by experts who can ensure the process aligns with your values. Hiring a professional can keep your planning project on track and ensure it is completed on time and within budget, while reducing the burden on your existing staff.

Carefully considering the full costs of the process is an enlightening part of the strategic planning process. There are often skill and resource gaps between the current skill set of the organization and what is needed to complete the process. However, knowing these up-front costs, and the interest in creating a strong strategic plan, positions you to liaise with a donor who cares about your organization and will assist in funding the process.

Begin with Vision: The Planning Mindset

Before diving into data, spreadsheets, or SWOT analyses, start by dreaming big. Strategic planning is about daring to articulate where you truly want to go. Too often, nonprofit leaders begin their planning by looking at what resources they currently have instead of what impact they dream of achieving. I firmly believe that if you don't put your vision into words, it will never have the chance to become reality.

Every transformative plan begins with a simple question: *What could we do if we had the resources, support, and capacity to fully realize our mission?*

Don't censor your organization's aspirations because the budget isn't there yet or because it feels too bold. This is the time to think expansively. Later, you can adjust based on capacity, infrastructure, and funding. But first, give yourself permission to dream big, and to say it out loud.

This first stage of planning is about reflection and alignment. It allows your team to see whether your mission, vision, and values truly reflect who you are today and where you want to be tomorrow. It sets the stage for everything that follows in the Five Factors™ framework, because clarity of purpose informs how you measure outcomes, allocate resources, build teams, and engage donors.

Foundational Questions for Reflection

The following questions will help your organization assess its current state, clarify its purpose, and define a desired future. They are open-ended for a reason: they are designed to spark deep discussion, reveal assumptions, and highlight the gap between where you are and where you want to be. Use them in retreats, leadership discussions, or board sessions to lay the foundation for your strategic plan.

Understanding Who You Are

- What issue are you trying to solve? Be specific: are you solving world hunger or local hunger, helping kids graduate, or ensuring fish can make it upstream to spawn? Why is this important not only to your organization but also to society and the people you serve?
- What is your **mission statement**? Does it clearly express how your work drives change?
- What is your **vision statement**? If your mission succeeds, how will your community, or even the world, be different?
- What **values** guide your work? Do they shape how staff, volunteers, and clients experience your organization, and are they practiced from the top down?
- Who do you **serve**? Define your clients precisely. If you serve "youth," which youth? From what backgrounds, geographies, or circumstances? Are there overlooked audiences, such as partner organizations or referral sources, that should also be seen as "clients"?
- Who are your **funders**? Which individuals, foundations, or corporations are most aligned with your mission?

- What makes your organization **distinct** from others offering similar services? Why are you best positioned to address the need?
- How does your work create **lasting change** in individuals, communities, or systems? How do you prove this?

Envisioning the Future

Now, imagine your organization five years from today. This is your *Big Hairy Audacious Goal*—the future that inspires bold action. Don't let money drive this visioning process.

- What services will you be providing?
- What has grown: staff, sites, or communities served?
- What measurable change has your work created?
- How has your presence reshaped the ecosystem you serve?

Next, bring that vision closer to home. Think three years out. What must happen to move you toward that five-year picture?

- Budget growth and financial reserves
- Number of staff and key leadership positions
- Programs or initiatives operating successfully
- Milestones and accomplishments
- Facilities built or expanded
- Geographic reach or population served

By articulating these answers, you begin the true work of strategic planning as an act of aspiration grounded in purpose. Once you know where you want to go, the rest of the Five Factors™—Outcomes, Budget, Team, and Donors—can align around that destination.

Conducting an Environmental Scan

Once you have determined you are in an appropriate place in terms of where you really want to go, it's time to begin the next step of the strategic planning process. This next step in planning is understanding both where the organization is now and the environment it operates within. This process, often called an environmental scan, assesses internal capabilities and external forces that influence success. It lays the foundation for realistic goal setting.

An environmental scan is a critical step in strategic planning because it helps nonprofits understand both the internal and external factors that influence their success. A common tool is the SWOT analysis, which examines strengths, weaknesses, opportunities, and threats. Strengths and weaknesses are internal factors: skills, systems, reputation, and funding stability, while opportunities and threats come from outside forces such as policy changes, demographics, or economic shifts.

Gather input from multiple perspectives. Staff may highlight operational bottlenecks, while board members may see governance or funding challenges. Clients and partners can reveal service gaps or emerging needs. A well-rounded SWOT reflects the organization's full ecosystem. When done well, a SWOT analysis provides a balanced snapshot that helps nonprofits set realistic, mission-driven goals.

Step 1: Gather Input from Multiple Perspectives

A nonprofit's strengths and weaknesses typically look different depending on whom you ask. Board members, staff, volunteers, clients, and funders may all have valuable insights. To begin, collect feedback through surveys, focus groups, or one-on-one conversations. For example, staff may highlight internal workflow challenges, while board members may notice gaps in fundraising strategies. This inclusive approach ensures the SWOT reflects the lived realities of the organization.

Step 2: Identify Internal Strengths and Weaknesses

Strengths are the assets and capabilities that give the nonprofit an advantage. These might include a strong reputation in the community, dedicated staff, effective programs, or a diverse funding base. Weaknesses, on the other hand, are the internal challenges that hold the organization back, such as limited staff capacity, lack of updated technology, or dependence on a single funder. To make this part actionable, the team should ask of its numerous stakeholders: What do we do well? Where do we struggle? What resources or systems are lacking? Why do stakeholders choose us over similar organizations? Where are the gaps in our services?

Step 3: Scan the External Environment for Opportunities and Threats

Opportunities are external factors the nonprofit could leverage to grow or improve, such as new funding opportunities, shifting community needs, or potential partnerships. Threats are external risks that could hinder progress. Examples include changes in government policy, increased competition for grants, or economic downturns. Research, such as reviewing sector trends, speaking with funders, or analyzing community data (such as city reports on homelessness or Census data), helps identify these factors. Key questions to ask include: What external trends could benefit us? What external forces could harm us? Is there still a need for our organization? What do we see on the horizon?

Step 4: Map the Findings into the SWOT Grid

Once data is gathered, the team can organize it into a four-quadrant grid labeled Strengths, Weaknesses, Opportunities, and Threats. Keeping the list concise is important. Typically, aim for four to six points in each category when it comes to the final version. It is perfectly fine while brainstorming to create a longer list, but after working with various stakeholders, narrow it down to key findings. This makes the analysis easier to use when setting strategic priorities.

Step 5: Translate Insights into Action

A SWOT analysis is not just an exercise; its value comes from applying it. For example, if one strength is "a strong volunteer base" and one opportunity is "increased community interest in service projects," the nonprofit might set a goal to expand volunteer-led programming. Similarly, if a weakness is "limited financial reserves" and a threat is "potential government funding cuts," the strategic plan might prioritize building an operating reserve.

By following these steps, nonprofits can use a SWOT analysis to bridge the gap between *where they are* and *where they want to go*. It becomes a foundation for decision-making, ensuring that future goals are grounded in the organization's realities and external environment.

While the SWOT analysis is most common, there are numerous other options that can be used as a replacement or in tandem for a fuller understanding of where the organization stands. For example, a PEST or PESTLE analysis specifically examines these external components:

- Political: Government funding priorities, regulations, public policies affecting service delivery, and projected trends.
- Economic: Inflation, employment rates, interest rates, the stock market, and the financial health of communities served.
- Social: Demographic shifts, community attitudes, cultural changes, and public awareness of issues.
- Technological: Emerging tech, data systems, AI, and other impactful trends.
- Legal/Environmental (optional): Compliance requirements, environmental factors, or sustainability concerns.

The PEST/PESTLE analysis can be combined with a SWOT analysis, with the factors of PEST/PESTLE being considered. Calling attention to these specific components broadens the focus beyond internal operations to the larger ecosystem. It is a helpful tool in anticipating shifts that could impact funding, client needs, or program delivery.

Somewhat similar to a SWOT analysis is a SOAR analysis. However, it should be noted that SOAR is a more positive, future-oriented alternative to SWOT. Rather than focusing on threats and weaknesses, it emphasizes what's working and how to build on it. The SOAR analysis is focused on:

- Strengths: What the organization does best.
- Opportunities: Where growth or partnerships are possible.
- Aspirations: What the organization hopes to achieve or become.
- Results: What success will look like and how it will be measured.

A SOAR analysis can be helpful when thinking about future goals of the organization, but it should not be a replacement for a SWOT analysis, because some considerations for the environment the organization is operating in must be taken into consideration. A nonprofit can aspire to grow into operating in another country, but if there is no consideration taken for the legal and accounting challenges that may develop from the approach, the organization is setting itself up for failure.

Finally, a third and very popular option is Michael Porter's Five Forces Analysis. It is especially useful when you want to understand competition and collaboration in the field. The five forces are:

1. Competition among existing players (other nonprofits offering similar services)
2. Threat of new entrants (new organizations addressing the same issue)
3. Substitute services (alternatives to your programs, e.g., government services or private providers)
4. Bargaining power of funders (how dependent are you on a few large donors?)
5. Bargaining power of beneficiaries/clients (do clients have choices, or are you the only option?)

Porter's model is especially helpful when nonprofits are looking to carve out their niche and to confirm, or not, that their organization provides a valuable and needed service in the community. In other words, it can help you clarify your unique value proposition.

These models are not academic exercises; they ground your plan in evidence. By combining internal reflection with external analysis, nonprofits create a realistic picture of where they stand and what forces will shape their future. By carefully considering the internal and external factors influencing the organization, nonprofits are better positioned to set priorities that are achievable and relevant. Involving staff, board members, and community stakeholders in the process creates a more holistic picture of where the organization stands and what it must prepare for.

Including All Voices: From the Streets to the Boardroom

A plan built in isolation, by executives or staff alone, will always miss part of the truth. The strongest strategies come from listening to every voice that shapes your mission: staff, clients, volunteers, donors, and community partners. Each offers a unique lens on what's working and where change is needed.

Begin by mapping who your stakeholders truly are. Internally, that includes executives, managers, and frontline employees. Externally, it means donors, partners, and those most directly served by your programs. Each group experiences the organization differently and can reveal gaps others can't see.

For people receiving services, accessibility is key. Online surveys may exclude those without consistent internet or literacy skills. In-person conversations held where people already gather, such as shelters, community centers, or events, often yield more authentic feedback. Providing food, transportation, or small stipends shows respect for their time and helps deepen trust.

For staff, anonymity typically encourages honesty. Anonymous surveys or facilitated discussions led by neutral moderators can surface real challenges that leadership might otherwise overlook, such as communication breakdowns, burnout, or inequities.

For board members and donors, engagement should go beyond oversight to shared vision. Structured interviews or retreats help align aspirations with the needs identified by staff and clients. When board members see planning as a learning opportunity rather than a formality, their advocacy and commitment grow.

Whatever method you choose, ensure accessibility. Keep surveys short and readable, use adaptive-friendly formats, and focus on open-ended questions that invite genuine responses rather than pre-set options. The goal isn't to confirm what you already believe. It's to hear the truth.

When done well, inclusive planning becomes a culture of listening. It builds trust, transparency, and collective belief in the mission, ensuring your plan is not just written *about* your community but *with* it.

Choosing the Right Engagement Tool

Once you've identified who needs to be at the table, the next step is deciding *how* to engage them. Different groups respond best to different approaches. What works for board members won't always resonate with clients or volunteers. The goal is to choose tools that make participation easy, comfortable, and authentic. Whether through surveys, interviews, focus groups, or community listening sessions, each method has strengths and limitations. What matters most is that every voice has a chance to be heard in a way that feels respectful and real.

Surveys

Surveys are efficient tools for collecting honest, anonymous input, especially when responses are needed from many people in a short time. Keep them five minutes or less to avoid drop-off. They can be tailored for different audiences:

- **Board and Staff:** Ask about organizational strengths, weaknesses, challenges, and opportunities. Staff often identify operational issues that leadership may not see.
- **Donors or Funders:** Explore what inspires their support, how they perceive transparency, and whether the organization communicates effectively.
- **Clients or Participants:** Assess satisfaction with services, identify unmet needs, and gather ideas for improvement.

Focus Groups

Focus groups provide deeper insights by encouraging discussion among a small group of participants. They allow people to build on one another's ideas and reveal perspectives that may not surface in written surveys. Comfort and trust are key. Participants are more open when they feel safe and heard. A skilled facilitator helps keep the discussion balanced and on track, probing for clarity and avoiding dominance by one voice. Focus groups can also be used after surveys to explore themes in more depth or to test new ideas before implementation.

Community Feedback Sessions

These are open forums where a broader community can share its views on organizational direction and needs. They can be structured around questions such as "What gaps in services do you see in our community?" or "How can we make a greater impact?" While these sessions foster transparency and trust, they can also veer off-topic or be dominated by strong personalities. Professional facilitation helps ensure productive, inclusive discussions.

One-on-One Interviews

Personal interviews yield detailed, candid feedback that other methods may miss. They are particularly valuable for engaging key stakeholders such as board members, major donors, longtime clients, community leaders, or partners. Advantages include:

- **Depth:** Interviews uncover nuance and new ideas.
- **Relationship Building:** They show respect and build trust through personal connection.
- **Clarification:** Interviewers can probe deeper or clarify statements in real time.
- **Safety:** Individuals often share sensitive feedback more freely in private.

Challenges include time demands and potential bias, since interviews reach fewer people and can overrepresent certain groups if not balanced intentionally.

Using a combination of methods ensures a richer, more representative understanding of the organization. Surveys provide breadth, while focus groups and interviews offer depth. Open forums strengthen transparency and accountability. To make participation equitable, offer flexible formats: online and in-person options, translation services, and sessions held at convenient times and locations. Finally, close the feedback loop by showing participants how their input shaped the final plan. This transparency builds trust and reinforces that every voice, from clients to board members, truly matters.

Analyzing Data to Build Strategic Clarity

Without intentional analysis, valuable insights remain scattered, and plans risk being built on assumptions rather than evidence. Turning raw information into understanding is where strategy begins to take shape. This stage is about finding meaning in the details—identifying patterns, connecting themes, and translating data into insights that drive action and alignment across the organization.

Start by consolidating all sources of input into one place: survey results, focus group notes, interviews, financial data, and performance metrics. Look for patterns rather than isolated comments. Which challenges surface repeatedly across different groups? Where do perspectives align, and where do they diverge? Do they vary by stakeholder type or demographic? For example, staff may highlight resource shortages while board members focus on governance or donor engagement. Both viewpoints are valid and, together, reveal the connection between internal capacity and external expectations.

Group findings into broad themes such as programs, operations, funding, leadership, and culture. This turns hundreds of individual data points into a clear, cohesive picture.

Next, quantify what you can. Even qualitative feedback, like open-ended survey comments, can be categorized and counted to reveal trends. If 60% of staff mention communication gaps, that signals an urgent internal priority. Visual tools such as charts, dashboards, and word clouds make patterns easier to interpret and share. Pair these summaries with a few representative quotes to preserve the human voice behind the numbers.

Once your analysis reveals the story behind the data, the next step is communicating it to turn insight into influence. How you share findings determines whether your results inspire understanding, spark change, and unite stakeholders around a shared path forward.

Communicating the Data

Survey analysis identifies strengths, risks, and opportunities, but communication determines whether those insights are integrated into the organization's operating reality. Clear reporting enables boards, leadership, and staff to interpret findings consistently and move forward with accountability. To close the loop, share what you learned and how feedback shaped the final plan. This step, so often skipped, turns participation into partnership. When people see their words reflected in the results, they take ownership of the outcome and become invested in what comes next.

Communicate findings strategically and with intention. The goal isn't to overwhelm stakeholders with data, but to show them what the information *means*. How it informs direction, addresses concerns, and guides decisions. Whether presenting to staff, board members, donors, or community partners, frame results in a way that reinforces trust: you listened, you learned, and you're building the plan with them in mind.

For board members, focus on high-level insights and implications for governance and long-term sustainability. Summarize trends in community need, the funding landscape, and organizational performance. Present clear takeaways based on what the data suggests the board must prioritize, such as diversifying revenue, strengthening evaluation systems, or improving succession planning. Framing the analysis in terms of board responsibility invites their engagement in shaping solutions rather than reacting to problems.

For staff, transparency is essential. Share how their input contributed to the findings and highlight both strengths and areas for growth. Use team meetings or visual dashboards to review the key themes, emphasizing how this information will guide upcoming planning decisions. Encourage discussion around what surprised them, what they agree with, and what they think deserves further exploration. When staff see that their voices were heard and are shaping the path forward, trust and ownership increase.

It's equally important to align the language and framing of the analysis with your organization's culture. Keep the tone balanced. Acknowledge challenges honestly, but also highlight successes and opportunities. Data can be a unifying force when it is presented not as a critique but as a shared foundation for progress.

Use this phase to set communication norms for the planning process. Create a cadence for sharing updates: monthly internal summaries, quarterly board reports, and periodic community updates. A simple communication plan outlining who receives which information, how often, and in what format will keep everyone engaged and informed as planning moves forward.

By analyzing and communicating data thoughtfully, the organization moves from collecting information to creating shared understanding. This process bridges the gap between diverse perspectives and builds alignment around what truly matters. When stakeholders see their feedback reflected in clear, actionable insights, they become partners in shaping the strategy rather than passive recipients of a final plan.

Balancing Vision with Capacity: The Reality Check

Earlier in the planning process, you were encouraged to dream boldly—to imagine what your organization could accomplish if resources were limitless. That exercise set the tone for possibility. Now comes the reality check. To turn big ideas into results, your vision must align with your actual capacity. A plan that inspires but ignores available time, funding, or staff will frustrate rather than empower.

This stage is about alignment. A strong plan should stretch your organization, but it must also honor current capacity. When goals exceed what your team or budget can sustain, even the best ideas falter. The task now is to prioritize: identify which goals will create the most meaningful impact now and which belong in a future phase. Doing fewer things exceptionally well will always deliver greater long-term results than pursuing too many at once.

Assess capacity in three key areas: financial, human, and operational. Ask hard questions: Do we have the funding to support these initiatives? Do we have the right team in place, or must we hire or train? Are our systems and processes strong enough to handle growth? A nonprofit with a $500,000 budget cannot realistically launch five new programs in three years without first expanding revenue and staffing. Likewise, a small team cannot scale services statewide without strengthening operations and volunteer infrastructure.

This isn't about limiting ambition, but rather it is about sequencing it wisely. Growth happens not through doing everything at once, but through sustained focus on a few well-chosen priorities executed with excellence. The goal is to determine whether your organization has the resources, systems, and leadership to carry out the plan, and if not, what needs to be strengthened first. Begin by evaluating three core areas: financial capacity, human capacity, and operational capacity.

Financial Capacity

Ask:

- Do we have the financial reserves to take calculated risks or weather setbacks?
- Are our funding streams diverse and reliable, or do we depend on one or two sources?
- Do we have the financial reporting systems and dashboards needed for real-time decision-making?
- How accurate and accessible are our financial projections?

Systems to review:

- Accounting and budgeting software
- Internal financial controls and reporting structures
- Grant management and fundraising tracking systems
- Reserve and investment policies

If the organization's cash flow is tight or dependent on short-term grants, build stability first. Expand multi-year funding, strengthen donor relationships, or invest in financial systems before launching major initiatives.

Human Capacity

Ask:

- Do we have enough staff and volunteers to execute this plan without overextending?
- Are the right people in the right roles, with clear responsibilities?

- Is our leadership team aligned and capable of managing growth?
- How are we supporting professional development and retention?
- Are we ready to release staff whose skill set no longer meets the needs of the organization?

Systems to review:

- Organizational chart and job descriptions
- Staff workload analysis
- Volunteer recruitment and management systems
- Performance management and professional development plans

If capacity gaps exist, determine whether to hire, train, or partner with others. Growth requires not just more people, but the right people equipped to lead effectively. This is a critical issue for many nonprofits as they grow from an "everyone does everything" to needing specialists or individuals with more advanced experience.

Operational and Infrastructure Capacity

Ask:

- Do our systems and tools support efficiency and scalability?
- Are our data, technology, and communication systems reliable and secure?
- Can our physical space or digital infrastructure handle expansion?
- Do we have clear processes for program delivery, evaluation, and decision-making?

Systems to review:

- Donor management (CRM) and client tracking databases
- IT infrastructure, cloud storage, and cybersecurity measures
- Facilities and space utilization
- Policies for project management, communications, and evaluation

Infrastructure gaps often limit impact more than funding. Before expanding services or launching new initiatives, ensure the behind-the-scenes systems are strong enough to sustain the growth you envision. Once you've examined each area, summarize findings in a capacity matrix, rating your organization's strength in each category on a scale of one to five. This provides a clear visual of where you are ready to grow and where you must build first.

Use these findings to sequence your goals. If your organization has strong staff but weak systems, prioritize technology or infrastructure improvements before launching a major expansion. If funding is solid, but leadership is stretched thin, invest in team development before adding programs.

By pairing your big dreams with realistic assessments and actionable priorities, you position your organization not just to grow, but to grow well, with the strength and systems to sustain impact long into the future.

> **The Emotional Side of Growth**
>
> Strategic growth is not just a technical process, but it's also quite an emotional one. As organizations evolve, leaders often face hard choices that touch on loyalty, history, and identity. You may find yourself needing to restructure teams, redefine long-standing roles, or let go of beloved "do-it-all" staff who were instrumental in building the organization but may not have the skill sets needed for the next phase. Similarly, legacy programs that once embodied your mission may need to end if they no longer produce meaningful impact or align with strategic priorities.
>
> These decisions can be painful, creating feelings of loss, guilt, and even resistance from those who care most about the mission. The key is to approach transitions with empathy and transparency, honoring the contributions of those who came before, clearly communicating the reasons for change, and emphasizing that these shifts are made to strengthen the organization's long-term ability to serve. Growth requires courage, not just strategy, and leading through these moments with compassion builds trust that lasts far beyond the transition itself.

Putting It All Together: Building Your Plan on Paper

After months of dreaming, data gathering, and reflection, it's time to bring your plan to life on paper. This stage marks a shift from exploration to creation. It's where your ideas start to take form, your direction becomes visible, and the team begins to see how their collective effort will move the organization forward. This is not your final, polished strategic plan. Instead, think of it as the *blueprint*, the framework that will guide the development of your detailed budget, measurable outcomes, and accountability systems in the next phase.

Step One: Forming the Planning Committee

Creating a plan this important should never fall on one person's shoulders. Begin by forming a planning committee: a small, balanced group that represents different perspectives within your organization. This team might include a few board members, senior staff, and possibly a trusted partner or advisor who can challenge assumptions and bring fresh insight. This process works best when facilitated by someone neutral, whether an internal leader who can balance voices or an outside consultant who brings objectivity.

Their job is to translate all the input you've collected, such as stakeholder feedback, capacity assessments, and SWOT results, into a clear and coherent direction. The group should approach this work with openness and curiosity, not as a bureaucratic exercise. The goal is to align around a shared understanding of what success looks like, what resources it will take to get there, and how to express that vision clearly enough to inspire others.

Step Two: Crafting the One-Page Strategic Overview

The first tangible product of the committee's work is a one-page strategic overview, a document that captures the essence of the organization's future in a simple, visual form. This page becomes your compass, the document you will return to again and again when priorities shift or opportunities arise.

This one-pager should include your mission, vision, and core values, and foundational questions you've been exploring throughout this process:

- Who are our clients or beneficiaries, and what needs do we meet?
- Who are our donors or funders, and why do they invest in us?
- What makes our organization unique? What is our "secret sauce"?
- What will success look like in three years?

Be specific when painting your three-year picture. Include measurable elements such as:

- How many clients or participants you will serve.
- How much staff you'll employ and in what roles.
- Your geographic reach: where you'll expand or deepen presence.
- Your annual operating budget and reserve goals.
- Key fundraising, partnership, or program achievements.

This one-page plan is your guidepost, not a marketing piece. It doesn't need to be perfect; it just needs to be clear. It's the statement of intent you'll refine and stress-test during later discussions and retreats.

Here is an example of what a one-page overview might look like:

Mission

Empower underserved youth and families in the Greater Metro area by providing comprehensive educational support, mentorship, and career readiness programs that foster lifelong learning, confidence, and opportunity.

Vision

A thriving community where every young person has equitable access to education, mentorship, and pathways to meaningful careers, breaking cycles of poverty and unlocking their full potential.

Culture

- Inclusivity: Every individual is valued and respected, regardless of background or circumstance.
- Collaboration: Staff, volunteers, families, and community partners work together to achieve shared goals.
- Innovation: Programs are continuously improved through feedback, creativity, and evidence-based practices.
- Accountability: Transparent operations and measurable outcomes guide all actions and decisions.
- Empowerment: Youth and families are supported to become leaders and advocates in their own lives and communities.

Strategic Overview

Who Are Our Clients or Beneficiaries, and What Needs Do We Meet?

Our clients are underserved youth and families in the Greater Metro area facing barriers to educational and economic opportunity. Needs met include after-school tutoring, college readiness, and career mentorship, building skills, confidence, and pathways to success.

Who Are Our Donors or Funders, and Why Do They Invest in Us?

Our donors include local businesses, private foundations, and individual philanthropists passionate about educational equity and community development. They invest due to our proven impact, transparent operations, and innovative, relationship-driven approach.

What Makes Our Organization Unique?

A holistic, relationship-driven model combining academic support, mentorship, family engagement, and real-world career exposure. Staff and volunteers build lasting relationships, creating a supportive community that fosters long-term growth.

What Will Success Look Like in Three Years?

- Fundraising revenue of $3,000,000.
- Serve 1,200 youth annually, up from 600, with expanded programming for middle and high school students.
- Grow to 18 full-time staff, including new roles in mental health support, college counseling, and community outreach.
- Deepen presence in the Metro area and expand to two neighboring counties, establishing satellite sites in each.
- Reach an annual operating budget of $2.5 million, with a reserve fund of $500,000.
- Secure three new multi-year foundation grants, launch a corporate partnership program, and pilot a youth internship initiative with local employers.
- Achieve a 95% high school graduation rate among participants, with 80% enrolling in post-secondary education or training.

Step Three: Defining the Next 12 Months

Once the committee agrees on the three-year picture, it's time to define what must happen in the next 12 months to keep you on course. The first year is about momentum. It should include the big wins that will set your organization up for success.

Start by estimating how much revenue you'll need to reach those goals. Then, break that total into earned income and fundraising targets. The more specific you can be, the more realistic your next steps will become.

Next, identify five to ten major outcomes that will make the biggest difference by year's end. These are not small operational tasks, but defining achievements that signal progress. Examples might include:

- Hosting a signature fundraising event that adds 100 new attendees and generates $500,000 in new revenue.
- Hiring a development director to expand major gifts and sponsorships.
- Opening a second program location serving 150 new clients.
- Establishing a three-month operating reserve through multi-year funding.
- Launching a pilot program that produces measurable community impact.

These annual milestones give your team focus and help you test whether your ambitions align with your current capacity.

Annual Plan
To be accomplished by: / /

Budget goal		
Fundraising goal		
Reserve goal		
Earned revenue		
Operational Goals		
List what you will have accomplished toward your three-year goal by this time next year	*Target date*	*Who is responsible*

Step Four: Setting 90-Day Action Cycles

With your one-year goals in place, it's time to create the rhythm that keeps the plan moving forward: 90-day action cycles. These quarterly windows are short enough to maintain urgency, but long enough to achieve meaningful progress.

For each 90-day period, the planning committee should answer three questions:

1 What must be accomplished in the next 90 days to reach our annual milestones?
2 Who will take the lead on each action?
3 How will we measure success?

The emphasis here is on what is *critical*, not everything that could be done. These are your "must-do" priorities: the tasks that will either move the organization forward or hold it back if delayed.

For example:

- Finalize the sponsorship structure and marketing plan for the gala.
- Complete hiring for two new staff positions.
- Launch a quarterly donor engagement newsletter.
- Implement a new CRM system for tracking program impact.

At the end of each quarter, review what was completed, celebrate progress, and adjust the next 90-day plan based on lessons learned. This steady cadence of review and realignment keeps the plan alive and adaptable.

90-Day Action Steps
To be accomplished by: / /

Budget goal		
Fundraising goal		
Reserve goal		
Earned revenue goal		
Operational Goals		
List what your team has to do in the next 90 days to get to your one-year goal	*Target date*	*Who is responsible*

Step Five: Holding a Strategic Planning Retreat

Once the one-page vision, annual milestones, and first set of 90-day priorities are drafted, it's time to bring the broader leadership together. A strategic planning retreat allows the full board, senior staff, and other key partners to engage deeply with the work.

The retreat is both a checkpoint and a catalyst. It provides space to:

- Review and refine the draft plan together.
- Ensure the mission, values, and vision resonate across the organization.
- Gather input on priorities and sequence.
- Build collective ownership of the plan's direction.

The tone of the retreat should be collaborative and forward-looking. Use visuals, discussion prompts, and scenario exercises to keep energy high and dialogue productive. The most effective retreats strike a balance between strategic depth and inspiration, and remind participants *why* this work matters while grounding them in practical next steps.

By the end of the retreat, you should leave with three things:

1 Agreement on the three-year vision and first-year priorities.
2 Input on what resources or adjustments may be needed to achieve first-year priorities.
3 Commitment from leaders and staff to move into the budgeting and outcomes phase.

Not every three-year goal will have a clear action item right away, and that's perfectly normal. Sometimes, the next step isn't to act, but to learn. A goal may require stepping back to gather information, pilot a concept, or secure funding before moving forward. For example, expanding to a new region might first require conducting a feasibility study or community needs assessment. Launching a new program could start with a small pilot to test assumptions and evaluate outcomes before scaling. In these cases, "planning to plan" is a strategic move, not a delay. It ensures that future actions are based on evidence, capacity, and readiness rather than assumptions. Building in time for research, testing, and evaluation helps avoid costly missteps and leads to stronger, more sustainable outcomes when implementation begins.

This working plan, your one-page strategic overview, one-year milestones, and 90-day cycle are the foundation for everything that follows. It's the blueprint for building your budget, setting measurable outcomes, and developing an accountability chart that ties people, processes, and performance together.

The collaborative, iterative, and inclusive process of getting here lays the groundwork for long-term success. It ensures your organization is not just writing a plan, but building the mindset and systems to carry it out. As you move into the next phase, remember: this is the start of a journey. The big dream you defined early in this chapter hasn't gone anywhere, it's now structured, prioritized, and ready to grow into reality.

Establishing Accountability

Accountability transforms a plan from paper into practice. Every goal, milestone, and action step must have a clearly defined owner and measurable result. It is not enough to say, "The goal is complete." Success must be visible, something tangible you can point to and say, *this happened because of our plan*. That might mean a program launched, a report published, a partnership agreement signed, or a revenue milestone reached. Tangible deliverables create shared understanding across teams so that once a task is delegated, everyone knows exactly what success looks like.

When setting success metrics, focus on what can be observed, verified, or counted, not just what can be discussed. For example, "launch a new youth mentorship program and enroll 50 students" is far more actionable than "expand youth services." This level of clarity reduces confusion, prevents tasks from stalling, and enables leaders to track real progress over time.

Best practice is to embed accountability into your organizational rhythm. Quarterly check-ins or dashboard reviews keep goals top of mind and allow for quick course corrections. Each review should answer three questions: What have we accomplished? What remains? What barriers need to be addressed? These sessions build alignment, surface challenges early, and reinforce a culture of transparency.

Finally, accountability extends beyond internal operations. Communicating outcomes, both wins and setbacks, with staff, board, and donors demonstrates integrity and builds trust. Funders, in particular, value organizations that measure and share impact honestly. A plan grounded in clear deliverables and visible results signals professionalism, reliability, and readiness for growth.

Evaluating and Updating the Plan

A strong strategic plan should never be static; it should be *evergreen*. The most effective plans evolve with the organization and its environment, staying relevant through both challenges and successes. Flexibility is not a weakness; it is a defining strength of good planning.

Circumstances will change: funding priorities shift, natural disasters occur, leadership transitions happen, and sometimes programs simply don't work as intended. When these moments arise, a well-built plan allows you to adjust course without losing sight of your long-term vision.

Regular review cycles, quarterly for short-term goals and annually for the big picture, keep the plan alive. These sessions are opportunities to evaluate progress, troubleshoot obstacles, and reframe timelines as needed. The process of setting 90-day and annual goals, then revisiting them regularly, ensures your strategy remains active rather than forgotten in a binder. It's also a time to identify emerging opportunities and pivot quickly when something accelerates your success.

One client received an unexpected $3 million gift midway through their three-year plan. Because their strategy was solid and well aligned, they didn't need to rewrite it, they simply accelerated implementation, completing in two years what they had anticipated would take three. A well-structured plan should withstand both setbacks and windfalls, guiding the organization forward with clarity and confidence.

The key is to anchor flexibility in data. Decisions about adjusting goals, timelines, or investments should be informed by measurable outcomes, not just intuition. Regular evaluation based on metrics, such as clients served, funds raised, or outcomes achieved, provides a clear picture of what's working and what needs refinement. When treated as a living, responsive tool rather than a one-time exercise, your plan becomes more than a document; it becomes the heartbeat of your organization's growth and resilience.

Case Study: The Future of Chiropractic

By the late 2010s, the chiropractic profession found itself at a crossroads. While millions of people relied on chiropractic care for pain management and wellness, the field lacked a shared, data-driven strategy and struggled to present a unified voice. Competing philosophies, fragmented organizations, and limited coordination around research and public education left the profession vulnerable to marginalization by other health disciplines. Recognizing this, leaders across the chiropractic ecosystem, representing state associations, colleges, practitioners, researchers, and corporations, came together at the 2019 ChiroCongress convention to chart a new path forward.

What began as a conversation evolved into one of the most inclusive strategic planning efforts in the history of the profession. In 2020, the Future of Chiropractic Visioning and Strategic Planning Project, now known as Chiropractic Future, was launched with a bold aim: to create a comprehensive, evidence-based roadmap that could guide the profession's growth for the next 50 years. The organizers understood that no single institution or personality could lead such an undertaking; it would require collective ownership and a process grounded in listening, data, and transparency.

The first phase of the project focused on information gathering. Over the course of a year, nearly 4,000 individuals from every corner of the chiropractic world participated through surveys, interviews, and focus groups. Practitioners from different philosophical backgrounds, academic researchers, policy advocates, students, and patients all contributed perspectives. The goal was to identify the field's shared values, strengths, and barriers. This broad participation not only provided valuable insights but also created a sense of unity among stakeholders who had historically worked in silos. Out of this process emerged a collective understanding of what chiropractic could become if guided by a clear and common plan.

In the second phase, participants transitioned from visioning to action. Volunteers were organized into four working groups: Legislation, Professional Identity, Research, and Utilization, each charged with defining long-term objectives and near-term actions. These groups met regularly to articulate five-year, three-year, and one-year goals, supported by concrete 90-day action steps. Each step had clear accountability, deadlines, and measurable outcomes. By grounding the process in data and structured implementation, the project ensured that the plan would not sit idle on a shelf but would instead drive real progress.

Several strategic priorities emerged. The first was to unify the profession's identity under the principle of "unity without uniformity," allowing for philosophical diversity while establishing a shared narrative about the value of chiropractic care. The second was achieving parity in compensation and recognition with other medical professions, an essential step in ensuring the field's sustainability. Other goals included expanding the research pipeline to strengthen the evidence base, increasing access and utilization of chiropractic services through public and private partnerships, and advocating for legislative changes around Medicare, Medicaid, and regulatory policy.

The final plan, covering 2021 through 2026, established a strong governance and implementation structure. Six standing committees were created: ChiroTech Consortium, Fundraising, Government Affairs, Intra-professional Communications, Public-facing Communications, and Research. Since its inception, the Reimbursement Committee and the Better Access to Chiropractic PAC have also been formed, each led by volunteers who had participated in the planning process. These committees were charged with carrying the plan forward, developing budgets, setting measurable outcomes, and coordinating across the field. Oversight was provided by a Strategic Plan Leadership Committee, ensuring accountability and alignment among the various efforts.

From the outset, the project embedded sustainability and transparency into its DNA. Fundraising was built into the plan rather than treated as an afterthought, ensuring that early wins could be translated into long-term capacity. Public updates, progress reports, and volunteer opportunities kept engagement high. Since implementation, the initiative has raised nearly $2 million in donations and in-kind contributions, logged over 10,000 volunteer hours, and garnered the formal support of hundreds of organizations and individuals. These metrics reflected not only financial success but also deep professional buy-in.

The impact of this planning process has been profound. The profession gained a cohesive voice, stronger research infrastructure, and greater visibility in health policy discussions. By emphasizing collaboration across differences, the Future of Chiropractic Project showed that strategic planning can do more than guide operations, it can transform culture. The plan's structure also demonstrated how to move from vision to measurable results, using volunteer-led committees and 90-day tactical plans to keep momentum alive.

For other nonprofits, the Future of Chiropractic Project offers an instructive model. It illustrates how inclusive planning can bridge divides, build ownership, and sustain engagement over time. By inviting participation from every level, practitioners, educators, funders, and beneficiaries, the project built both legitimacy and longevity. Its success reinforces a central lesson of strategic planning: when an organization invests in shared vision, structured accountability, and transparent communication, it not only strengthens its internal operations but also reshapes how an entire sector defines its future.

Turning a Strategic Plan into Branding

A completed strategic plan should never be a document that lives only on a shelf or in a shared drive; it is one of your organization's most powerful branding tools. Once finalized, the plan should be actively used and shared to communicate who you are, where you are going, and how others can join you in that journey. It provides a clear, compelling narrative for funders, investors, partners, and staff alike, showing not only the impact you've achieved but also the vision you're building toward.

A well-crafted plan clarifies your mission, priorities, and goals, creating a consistent message about your organization's purpose and direction. It becomes the foundation for all external communication: grant proposals, investor decks, fundraising appeals, media outreach, and even staff recruitment. Donors and partners are increasingly drawn to organizations that can articulate a confident, data-driven path forward. Sharing your plan demonstrates transparency, competence, and long-term vision, qualities that inspire trust and investment.

Your plan also serves as a storytelling framework. Each section, from the mission and values to the three-year goals, can be translated into language that strengthens your brand voice. It helps ensure that your marketing materials, website content, and social media posts all reinforce the same core identity. When what you say aligns perfectly with what you do, your brand becomes authentic, recognizable, and credible.

Internally, the plan should guide daily operations. Staff can reference it to prioritize work, make decisions, and align efforts across departments. For board members, it becomes a governance tool, clarifying what success looks like and how progress will be measured. For leadership, it becomes a touchstone for decision-making, ensuring that opportunities are evaluated against the strategic direction rather than short-term pressures.

Externally, your plan should be shared broadly with major donors, community partners, and even the general public. Including a polished, summarized version in investor packets or annual reports sends a strong message: We know where we're going, and we have a plan to get there. One client shared their three-year plan with funders during meetings, using it as both a communication piece and a visual roadmap; it became one of their most effective fundraising tools because it showed discipline, direction, and momentum.

In short, your strategic plan is your organization's brand narrative in action. When used deliberately, it communicates vision, builds confidence, attracts resources, and unites everyone, from board to community, around a shared future.

Putting Your Plan into Motion

Now that you've explored what effective planning really looks like, and why it's essential to every other factor in your organization's success, it's time to put the ideas into action. The following *Planning Process Preparation Checklist* is designed to help you gather the information, people, and tools you'll need to move from concept to execution.

Use it as your starting point before scheduling a retreat, engaging a consultant, or launching your next strategic planning process. Completing this preparation will ensure that when you sit down to plan, you're not guessing. You're building from a strong foundation of data, insight, and alignment.

Planning Process Preparation Checklist

This checklist walks you through what to collect, organize, and decide as you begin the Five Factor planning process.

1 Clarify Mission, Vision, and Goals

- ☐ Current mission and vision statements (review for clarity and relevance)
- ☐ Any strategic goals or priorities from past plans

- ☐ A draft or working "big dream" statement—what success looks like five to ten years out?
- ☐ Notes on how the organization defines success and impact today
- ☐ Key questions to guide discussion:
  - Are we solving the problem or managing it?
  - How will the world look different if we succeed?

---

2 Gather Core Organizational Information

- ☐ Organizational chart and staff roles/responsibilities
- ☐ List of current programs and services, including who they serve and what they provide
- ☐ Recent annual reports, budgets, and audits
- ☐ Board list and current committee structure
- ☐ Policies and procedures that guide operations

---

3 Collect Program and Outcome Data

- ☐ List of all programs with their intended outcomes
- ☐ Available inputs (resources, enrollments, or participation counts)
- ☐ Outputs (services delivered, workshops held, meals served, etc.)
- ☐ Outcomes (changes in knowledge, behavior, or condition)
- ☐ Data sources and systems used to track this information
- ☐ Gaps or missing data to address

Use your existing grant reports, client databases, or external research to fill in missing outcomes.

---

4 Assess Financial Health

- ☐ Current organizational budget and breakdown by program
- ☐ Three-year trend data on income and expenses
- ☐ Funding mix (grants, donations, earned income, contracts)
- ☐ True cost of service delivery by program (unit cost analysis)
- ☐ Reserves and debt status
- ☐ Current fundraising plan and major donor prospects

You'll use this data later to connect funding to strategy and determine sustainability.

---

5 Engage Key Stakeholders

- ☐ List of internal stakeholders (board, staff, volunteers)
- ☐ List of external stakeholders (funders, partners, community leaders, clients)
- ☐ Plan for how and when to gather their input (surveys, focus groups, interviews)
- ☐ Communication plan for keeping them updated throughout the process

The best plans are built with—not for—your stakeholders.

---

6 Analyze the Environment

- ☐ SWOT or landscape analysis (strengths, weaknesses, opportunities, threats)
- ☐ List of peer or competitor organizations and their differentiators

- ☐ Community needs assessment data or recent reports
- ☐ Policy or funding changes that may affect your mission

---

7 Define the Process and Timeline

- ☐ Appoint a planning lead or committee
- ☐ Decide who will facilitate (internal team, consultant, or hybrid)
- ☐ Outline timeline and milestones (visioning, data gathering, goal setting, writing)
- ☐ Determine how progress will be communicated and approved
- ☐ Schedule time for board and staff retreats or working sessions

---

8 Set Up Tools and Templates

- ☐ Create a shared planning folder (digital or physical)
- ☐ Set up working documents for goals, outcomes, and budgets
- ☐ Identify data visualization or dashboard tools to support outcomes tracking
- ☐ Prepare facilitation materials (agendas, surveys, slide decks, note templates)

---

9 Establish How You'll Measure Success

- ☐ Draft a preliminary logic model or outcome map
- ☐ Identify key metrics aligned with your Five Factors™
- ☐ Plan for annual review and adjustment of the plan

---

10 Communicate and Launch

- ☐ Plan how to share the final plan internally and externally
- ☐ Create talking points and visuals for board, funders, and donors

Summary—Clarity Creates Momentum

Nonprofits often find themselves stuck in cycles of fatigue, unclear direction, and reactive decision-making. Without a clear strategic plan, staff burn out, boards disengage, and donors lose confidence. The result is a constant struggle to stay afloat, scrambling for last-minute funding, weathering crises without a roadmap, and missing opportunities for meaningful growth. Strategic planning changes that. It provides the structure and clarity needed to align teams, attract investment, and navigate uncertainty with confidence. A thoughtful plan transforms an organization from surviving year to year into one that is steadily building toward long-term impact.

Today's donors act like investors. They look for organizations with vision, measurable results, and the infrastructure to scale. Transformative philanthropists have demonstrated that large, unrestricted gifts flow to nonprofits with proven capacity, sustainability, and clear strategies for growth. A well-developed plan communicates discipline, direction, and the ability to turn funding into measurable outcomes. The organizations that thrive are those that can show not just passion for their mission, but a concrete plan for achieving it.

Creating such a plan requires listening to every voice: staff, board, clients, and community alike. Engaging all stakeholders ensures that the strategy reflects real needs and opportunities, not just internal assumptions. This participatory approach builds buy-in and accountability, making implementation smoother and more authentic. It also strengthens fundraising: when donors see that those most affected by the mission helped shape the plan, they view the organization as credible, inclusive, and impact-driven.

Fundraising is strongest when it becomes a shared endeavor, not a top-down transaction. When clients, community partners, and donors all feel ownership in the mission, the relationship shifts from "support us" to "join us." Donors who are invited into advisory conversations, site visits, or pilot initiatives gain a firsthand understanding of the organization's value, and are far more likely to make transformative, long-term commitments. This inclusive approach builds a resilient funding ecosystem where multiple voices contribute to stability and growth.

Ultimately, a strategic plan is more than an internal document, it is both a management tool and a branding platform. It tells a unified story of who the organization is, what it stands for, and where it is headed. When shared with donors, partners, and the broader community, it projects confidence and credibility. A plan that is actionable, adaptable, and alive not only guides daily decisions, it inspires investment, builds trust, and fuels the kind of long-term change that nonprofits exist to create.

Key Takeaways

- **Start with vision, not limits.** Dream big before you edit down. Clarity grows from courage.
- **Engage your team early.** Planning isn't a solo exercise; it's a process that builds shared ownership.
- **Turn plans into action.** Translate every goal into specific, measurable steps and timelines.
- **Stay flexible.** Great plans evolve; use check-ins and dashboards to course-correct.
- **Plans inspire confidence.** Donors fund organizations that know where they're headed and why.

Progress Check

After reading this chapter, rate where your organization is on a scale of one to five, with one being that your organization does not have this component or is just beginning to work on it, and five meaning your organization is fully operational and has this element ready for vetting by a major donor.

Notes:

Citations

1 Unfortunately, according to BoardSource's latest Leading with Intent report (2021), only 29% of nonprofits surveyed reported that they had a written succession plan in place. Whether a transition occurs due to an unexpected vacancy on the staff or board, or the anticipated transition of a long-tenured leader, being deliberative and thoughtful, and having a plan in place, can help a nonprofit weather the inevitable challenges of leadership transition. Leading with Intent: BoardSource Index of Nonprofit Board Practices (Washington, DC: BoardSource, 2021) https://leadingwithintent.org/.

2 C. Wick & A. Parada (2020). National Assessment on the State of Fundraising for Domestic Violence Organizations.

3 "Friends of the Children receives $44 million from MacKenzie Scott." Philanthropy News Digest. August 26, 2022. https://philanthropynewsdigest.org/news/friends-of-the-children-receives-44-million-from-mackenzie-scott.

Chapter 2

Building Financial Health and a Strategic Budget

Donors and funders don't just want to know what you plan to do, but they want to know if you can actually do it. That starts with demonstrating sound fiscal health and a clear understanding of what it will cost to achieve your goals. This chapter is about building both financial health and a three-year fiscal roadmap. It's about connecting vision to resources, ensuring your organization has the people, systems, and funding to bring its plan to life.

Sustainable funding is essential for a nonprofit's long-term stability, enabling it to fulfill its mission without depending on sporadic, one-time gifts. A diverse mix of revenue—grants, individual donations, corporate sponsorships, and earned income—allows organizations to endure economic shifts and maintain critical programs even when certain funding streams fluctuate. Without financial sustainability, nonprofits face the constant risk of cutting services, losing staff, or closing their doors when donations decline.

A well-organized, sustainable budget is a prerequisite for most grant funding. Funders expect to see fiscal health and responsible management before making an award. They want to know that their investment will be used wisely and not lost to inefficiency or instability. Even after receiving a grant, renewal often depends on the organization's ability to demonstrate a realistic sustainability plan. Without one, funding may disappear as quickly as it arrived.

A strong financial foundation empowers nonprofits to plan strategically and invest in growth rather than reacting to crises. Reliable funding supports innovation, infrastructure improvements, and expanded community outreach. It also signals to donors and funders that the organization is credible, competent, and built for long-term impact. Financial sustainability is operationally necessary and a powerful trust signal that attracts investment and strengthens donor confidence.

DOI: 10.4324/9781003746218-3

Fear-Based Budgeting

If we're honest, most of us have looked at a realistic budget number and quietly trimmed it by a third, maybe even half, just to make the fundraising goal seem less daunting. We do it out of caution, not deceit, because we doubt our ability to raise the full amount or fear the pushback that comes with presenting the real number.

Fear-based budgeting occurs when an organization makes financial decisions driven by anxiety rather than strategy. It's the instinct to shrink the budget "just in case," to defer investments, or to freeze hiring, even when resources exist to support growth. While fiscal caution is a responsible practice, budgeting from a place of fear can quietly erode an organization's mission and momentum.

> Fear shrinks possibility. Strategy expands it.
>
> A courageous budget is not reckless—it's intentional, data-informed, and grounded in mission impact.

A fearful approach often leads to overly conservative spending, deferred maintenance, and hesitation to pursue new opportunities. Leaders may cut programs, delay technology upgrades, or reduce staff capacity, not because the organization lacks funds, but because they are uncertain about what the future holds. Over time, fear-based budgeting can create a self-fulfilling cycle of scarcity: by underinvesting in growth, organizations limit their ability to generate new revenue, attract top talent, or demonstrate capacity to major funders. Staff burnout rises as workloads increase and resources stagnate, while programs suffer from insufficient support. The result is an organization that appears cautious on paper but struggles to thrive in practice.

A healthier alternative is strategic budgeting, a balance of responsibility and courage. Strategic budgeting links financial choices directly to the *Plan* and *Budget* components of the Five Factors™ Framework, grounding every decision in data, impact, and mission alignment. It encourages leaders to take *calculated risks*: investing in capacity-building, fundraising systems, or talent development when the potential return justifies the expense.

Strategic budgeting prepares for uncertainty. By maintaining reserves, analyzing financial trends, and projecting multiple scenarios, an organization can remain stable while still pursuing growth. This approach replaces fear with foresight, allowing nonprofits to act from confidence rather than constraint. In doing so, they position themselves not just to survive financial challenges but to expand their reach and deepen their impact.

From Fear to Foresight—Shifting Your Budget Mindset

The following offers practical guidance for leaders and boards ready to move beyond a scarcity mindset. It outlines clear steps to replace fear-driven decision-making with data-informed, mission-aligned financial planning. Use it as a quick reference during budget discussions or board retreats to keep your organization focused on growth, sustainability, and impact rather than anxiety and restraint.

1 Anchor Every Dollar to the Plan

- Begin each budget cycle with your *strategic goals*, not last year's numbers.
- Ask: What does success look like, and what will it cost to achieve it?
- Align each expense to an objective in your plan to ensure spending supports mission outcomes.

2 Replace "What If" with "What's the Plan If"

- Fear-based questions start with *What if donations drop*?
- Strategic questions ask: What's our plan if donations drop?
- Build contingency scenarios and reserve policies that address uncertainty without paralyzing action.

3 Budget for Investment, Not Just Survival

- Allocate funds for staff training, technology, and fundraising systems—these are not luxuries but growth drivers.
- Identify areas where modest investments yield long-term returns in efficiency, sustainability, or revenue.

4 Use Data, Not Emotion, to Guide Decisions

- Review three-year financial trends before cutting or freezing expenses.
- Track cost-per-outcome metrics to understand which programs deliver the greatest impact for each dollar spent.
- Let data, not fear, define what's sustainable.

5 Communicate the "Why" Behind the Numbers

- Transparency builds confidence. Share with your board and donors how your budget advances the mission and manages risk.
- Use visuals and plain-language explanations to show how strategic investments strengthen outcomes and community impact.

6 Revisit and Adjust Regularly

- Conduct quarterly budget reviews and update projections as conditions change.

- Treat your budget as a living document, not a fixed rulebook.
- Celebrate when investments pay off. Success reinforces confidence in strategic risk-taking.

The Power of Multi-Year Planning

Many nonprofits build their budgets one year at a time, balancing revenue and expenses for the next 12 months, approving it, and moving on. While that annual process is necessary for operations, it is not sufficient for strategy. The reality is that year-to-year budget strategy won't cut it in today's environment. Economic conditions, grant cycles, and donor priorities shift constantly. Without a multi-year view, nonprofits are perpetually vulnerable to those fluctuations. They may appear stable on paper while quietly accumulating risk: unpredictable funding cycles, limited reserves, or infrastructure that can't scale with demand.

A long-term financial plan, spanning at least three years, transforms budgeting from an exercise in maintenance into a roadmap for mission fulfillment. It provides stability, direction, and foresight, allowing leadership to anticipate challenges, seize opportunities, and invest wisely.

A three- to five-year financial plan allows nonprofits to align money with mission. It links your strategic plan directly to your budget, ensuring that each goal, whether expanding services, upgrading technology, or launching a new program, is fully costed out and funded over time. For example, if you want to launch a new after-school program, how much will it cost to run this program, including extra administrative and fundraising expenses, insurance, and staffing? How will this be funded, and what is the cost per youth? This approach also builds credibility with funders, who increasingly prefer to invest in organizations that can demonstrate long-term financial vision and discipline. A nonprofit that can show how today's investments fuel impact over several years signals both competence and stability.

Multi-year planning also allows for smarter resource allocation. Instead of postponing capital needs or staff raises until a crisis hits, leadership can forecast costs, plan incremental growth, and build reserves in advance. A clear, forward-looking financial roadmap helps boards and funders understand not only what the organization needs now but also what it will take to sustain success in the years ahead.

How Long Should You Plan For?

For most nonprofits, a three-year financial plan strikes the right balance between flexibility and foresight. It provides enough time to implement the current strategic plan, pursue multi-year grants, and adjust to funding shifts. A five-year plan can offer a broader vision, which is ideal for organizations preparing for capital campaigns, large-scale program expansion, or major infrastructure investment. Plans beyond five years, such as endowment strategies or legacy giving, serve as aspirational roadmaps but should be reviewed regularly and updated based on new realities. At a minimum, your budget should cover the full cost of your current strategic plan.

Core Elements of a Strong Multi-Year Fiscal Plan

While every organization's context is unique, successful long-term financial planning typically includes:

- **Diversified Revenue Streams:** Avoid overreliance on a single funder or revenue type. Build a balanced mix of grants, individual gifts, corporate support, earned income, and investment returns to stabilize cash flow.
- **Operating Reserves:** Establish and maintain three to six months of operating expenses in reserve to protect against unexpected shortfalls or opportunities that require quick action.
- **Scenario Planning:** Develop best-case, moderate, and worst-case projections to prepare for funding fluctuations or economic downturns.
- **Strategic Investment in People and Infrastructure:** Budget for staff development, technology upgrades, and operational improvements that strengthen the organization's capacity, not just its programs.
- **Regular Review and Adjustment:** Revisit the plan annually to measure progress, refine assumptions, and adjust strategies based on performance and changing conditions.
- **Multi-Year Grant Positioning:** Pursue and design funding proposals that align with your long-term goals. Funders value consistency and often reward it with multi-year commitments.
- **Endowment and Planned Giving Development:** For mature organizations, long-term financial sustainability includes building permanent funding sources such as endowments or legacy gifts.

Estimating Your Revenue

Before you begin estimating expenses, it's essential to understand how your organization generates and sustains revenue. A strong budget doesn't start with what you spend, but rather with what you can realistically earn or raise. Estimating your revenue first ensures that your financial plan is grounded in reality, not aspiration. It's not about guessing what might happen; it's about building a credible financial roadmap based on evidence, history, and strategy.

A well-structured budget must also paint a clear picture of where revenue will come from and how dependable each source is. Understanding your revenue mix is essential not only for financial stability but also for determining your future campaign goals. A realistic revenue forecast allows you to test whether your plan is feasible and to identify where new fundraising, partnerships, or earned-income strategies will be required.

When developing a three-year budget, your revenue projections should be grounded in data, not optimism. The goal isn't to predict the future perfectly, but to create a working model that helps your team make informed decisions, assess risks, and plan for sustainable growth.

Step One: Identify Reliable Income Sources

Start by listing all current and anticipated revenue streams. This typically includes:

- Earned income: program fees, tuition, ticket sales, product sales, or social enterprise revenue.
- Government contracts and grants: local, state, or federal funding, ideally with multi-year commitments.
- Private philanthropy: individual donors, foundations, and corporate sponsorships.
- Investment or endowment income: predictable earnings, dividends, or interest revenue.

Label each source according to its level of reliability. Ask: *Can we count on this income with 80% confidence?* If not, classify it as "potential" rather than "confirmed." This discipline prevents overestimating revenue and gives you a clearer picture of what's truly secure.

Step Two: Use Historical Data and Trends

Review three to five years of financial history to identify patterns. Which sources have remained consistent? Which fluctuate year to year? Which have grown or declined? If a grant has been renewed for five consecutive years, it's likely dependable. If gala revenue has dropped annually, build that decline into your forecast. Grounding your projections in actual performance ensures your plan reflects reality rather than wishful thinking.

Step Three: Differentiate between Recurring and One-Time Income

A common budgeting mistake is assuming that last year's extraordinary gift or emergency grant will repeat. Distinguish recurring funding, like memberships, reimbursements, or regular donor pledges, from one-time opportunities, such as a special foundation grant or capital gift. The latter are valuable but should not fund ongoing operations. Instead, allocate them toward innovation, reserves, or capital improvements.

Step Four: Project Growth Responsibly

If your strategic plan calls for scaling programs, adding sites, or launching new initiatives, build conservative revenue assumptions around those efforts. Most new ventures take 12–18 months to stabilize income. Apply the same 80% confidence rule: if you can't reasonably count on a source, don't include it in your operating forecast. Flag it as "aspirational" revenue, which signals that new fundraising or business development will be required to achieve your goals.

Step Five: Connect Revenue to Campaign Planning

Your three-year revenue forecast becomes the foundation for your campaign planning. Once total projected expenses (operations, growth, and capital) are known, subtract your estimated revenue from that figure. The remaining balance represents your philanthropic goal: the amount you'll need to raise through private giving, grants, and partnerships.

This simple calculation transforms budgeting from a static accounting exercise into a strategic fundraising tool. It allows your leadership team, board, and donors to see the whole picture: what's funded, what's pending, and where their contributions make the greatest difference.

When done well, this process builds credibility. Donors are far more likely to invest when they see a clear, evidence-based financial plan with realistic projections and transparent gaps. Remember: strong campaign planning begins with strong financial forecasting. If your budget is grounded in truth, your fundraising case will be, too.

Cost of Doing Business

Once you've mapped out your likely revenue, the next step is to understand what it truly costs to deliver your mission. Every dollar earned or raised has to support a set of activities—programs, staff, infrastructure, and operational—that keep the organization running. Many nonprofits focus on bringing money in without fully understanding how much it takes to carry the work out. To build a sustainable budget, you must match revenue projections with a clear-eyed look at your expenses and the real cost of doing business.

I once worked with a nonprofit that charged $25 per class. When I asked about their profit margin, they looked puzzled. They had never calculated the true cost of delivery. Another organization proudly launched a retail product line but hadn't factored in staff time, overhead, or fulfillment costs to determine its actual margin. These aren't isolated cases; they're common nonprofit blind spots. Too often, organizations launch earned-income ventures or accept flat-fee government contracts without first testing whether those payments cover the real cost of service. The gap is then quietly filled by fundraising dollars, stretching the organization thinner and masking structural deficits.

The first step toward financial health is understanding what it truly costs to deliver your programs. Develop program-level budgets that break expenses into meaningful categories. For example, for a domestic violence shelter you would have costs for the facility, hotline, outreach, legal services, administration, and fundraising. Allocate shared costs such as insurance, technology, leadership salaries, and utilities proportionally across programs so each reflects its genuine share of overhead. Once you have this clarity, you can see which activities are sustainable, which need subsidy, and which may require rethinking entirely.

For-profit businesses rarely sell below cost. In fact, they build margins into every transaction to ensure growth and reinvestment. Nonprofits must adopt the same discipline. If counseling costs $100 per session, charging $25 may seem generous, but it creates an unsustainable deficit that eventually threatens service continuity. Financial sustainability means setting prices or reimbursement rates that reflect market realities, not out of greed, but out of respect for your staff, your mission, and your long-term survival.

Implementing sustainable pricing takes courage and time. Nonprofits must believe in the value of their work and confidently communicate that value. If a program or product cannot sustain itself at a fair price, that's valuable information. It may signal a need to adjust the model, explore new funding partnerships, or reassess community demand. And yes, shifting from free to fee-based services can cause temporary resistance. When I led an agency that offered professional training, we had long provided free sessions, even those offering continuing education credits (CEUs). Eventually, we began charging for private training while still offering one free community session every other month. At first, there was pushback, but soon, participants recognized that our offerings matched the quality of paid competitors charging hundreds of dollars. What had once been a cost center evolved into a reliable revenue stream that strengthened our mission.

One of my clients, a youth services provider, learned through a cost-per-unit analysis that they were losing nearly $60 per tutoring session under a state contract. Instead of absorbing the loss, the executive director used data to renegotiate. They presented evidence showing that reimbursement rates didn't even cover teacher salaries. The funder agreed to phased increases tied to documented outcomes. Within a year, the contract turned profitable, staff retention improved, and the agency's financial footing stabilized.

These examples illustrate a core principle of the Five Factors™ Framework: *Budget must align with both Plan and Outcomes.* Knowing your costs isn't just accounting; it's strategy. It informs program design, funding requests, and donor conversations. It also demonstrates professionalism and transparency, two qualities funders increasingly demand.

The takeaway is simple but powerful: nonprofits must stop undervaluing their work. By calculating the true cost of services, setting sustainable prices, and ensuring programs generate at least a modest surplus, organizations create the capacity to reinvest in their people, infrastructure, and innovation. Profitability in the nonprofit world doesn't contradict the mission; it preserves it. A strong financial model is what allows generosity to endure.

Calculating the True Cost

Understanding the true cost of service delivery is one of the most important steps toward financial sustainability. Too often nonprofits only calculate direct expenses, like staff time and materials, without accounting for the indirect or shared costs that keep programs running. The result is a distorted picture that makes services look more affordable than they really are, forcing fundraising to subsidize invisible deficits.

To uncover the real cost, begin by identifying direct costs, which are those that clearly belong to a specific program. This includes staff salaries, benefits, supplies, travel, or program-specific equipment. Next, allocate indirect costs, such as rent, utilities, technology, insurance, leadership salaries, and administrative support. These expenses should be distributed proportionally across all programs using a consistent method, such as the percentage of total staff time or square footage associated with the program, staff, or team members.

Once both sets of costs are assigned, calculate the true cost per unit of service using a simple formula:

(Direct Costs + Indirect Costs) ÷ Number of Service Units = True Cost per Unit

For example, if a counseling program costs $100,000 per year and delivers 1,000 sessions, the true cost of each session is $100. If the organization charges $25 per session or is reimbursed $40 through a contract, it operates at a loss of $60–$75 per session. These losses quickly accumulate across hundreds of sessions.

Knowing these figures allows leaders to make data-driven decisions: whether to adjust pricing, renegotiate reimbursement rates, or redesign service delivery. This clarity also helps build credibility with funders, who increasingly expect to see realistic, cost-based budgets tied to outcomes.

The goal isn't to eliminate low- or no-cost programs, but to make conscious choices about when and how to subsidize them. By clearly understanding unit costs, nonprofits can communicate the true value of their services, justify funding requests, and demonstrate stewardship. Transparency in pricing is about protecting the mission and ensuring the organization's capacity to continue serving for years to come.

Market-Rate Compensation

A strong budget begins with accurate assumptions, and one of the most important is compensation. To build a sustainable financial plan, nonprofits must understand what it truly costs to hire and retain talent in their market. That means researching salary benchmarks for every position, and not just guessing or basing decisions on what the organization can currently afford.

Market rates vary widely depending on geography, competition, and cost of living. A data entry clerk in New York City, for example, commands a very different wage and benefits than one in Tallahassee, Florida. Yet many nonprofits, desperate to stretch limited dollars, pay the absolute minimum they can. This short-term tactic often leads to long-term instability. When an organization underpays, it struggles to recruit qualified staff, loses good people to better-paying employers, and undermines the very mission it's trying to serve.

Paying below market rate also distorts the accuracy of a nonprofit's financial picture. If wages are set artificially low in the budget, the organization is building its financial model on a false foundation. Just as important, this principle applies beyond salaries. Rental spaces secured through a temporary discount, or professional services provided by a friend at a reduced rate, may not last. When those costs eventually rise to market value, as they inevitably do, the organization suddenly faces a budget crisis. A strong, honest budget reflects what things *should* cost, not what they currently do at a discount.

To build accurate budgets, nonprofits must include both realistic labor costs and market-rate inputs for goods and services. This ensures that financial projections are grounded in reality and that funding requests reflect the organization's true operational needs. Accounting for actual market rates helps nonprofits project future costs more accurately and make the case for what it genuinely takes to sustain impact.

Paying Fairly Is Strategic, Not Extravagant

Attracting and retaining talented, mission-driven employees is one of the most important investments a nonprofit can make. Yet many organizations, especially in the early years, underpay staff and offer minimal benefits, hoping that passion will compensate for pay gaps. This approach is both ethically problematic and financially shortsighted. Underpaid employees are more prone to burnout, leading to increased turnover. This results in a loss of institutional knowledge, consistency, and credibility for the organization. The process of recruiting and retraining new staff is both expensive and time-consuming, negatively impacting both financial resources and morale.

Offering competitive salaries and benefits is a sustainability strategy. Fair compensation builds loyalty, stability, and higher performance. It demonstrates to donors and partners that the organization values people as its greatest asset. Health insurance, retirement plans, paid leave, and professional development opportunities attract strong talent and signal long-term viability. While these benefits may feel out of reach, many states and local governments offer resources that can help. Some provide pooled insurance programs, workforce development grants, or capacity-building funds for leadership training. Even small steps, such as cost-sharing benefits or phased pay increases, can move an organization closer to true equity and sustainability.

Accurately Pricing Construction and Capital Projects

The same principle of honest pricing applies when budgeting for construction, renovation, or capital projects. Nonprofits often underestimate costs in an attempt to make a project appear more affordable to donors or the board of directors. They launch campaigns with optimistic budgets, only to discover mid-project that materials, labor, or permitting fees have far exceeded expectations. At that point, the organization must either scale back its vision or return to funders with an awkward request for additional support, which can damage trust and credibility. While donors may understand some unexpected increases, major missteps can cause the abrupt end of what could have been a very successful project.

Construction pricing should always reflect current market rates, not historical figures or best-case estimates. Prices fluctuate dramatically due to inflation, supply chain issues, labor shortages, and changes in code requirements. A responsible budget includes a contingency line item, typically 20–30% of total construction costs, to cover unforeseen expenses such as material delays, site issues, or design changes. It should also include the costs of a capital campaign fundraising strategy, such as donor events, staffing, and recognition. Skipping this step might make a budget look leaner, but it sets the organization up for embarrassment and financial strain.

For example, a nonprofit planning to build a community center might budget $2 million based on early contractor quotes. If those quotes fail to include rising steel prices or permit fees, and the true cost ends up at $2.4 million, the organization must scramble to raise another $400,000. Funders may question the organization's planning capacity, and confidence in future campaigns can suffer. Including realistic costs and contingencies from the start demonstrates professionalism and builds donor trust, even if the initial price tag feels uncomfortable.

A well-structured capital budget should include:

- Accurate, updated market estimates from multiple contractors.
- Soft costs such as design, permitting, inspections, and project management.
- Contingency (20–30%) for unforeseen issues.
- Inflation projections for multi-year projects.
- Fundraising and administrative costs.

Including these elements is responsible stewardship. Funders understand that construction costs rise, but what they don't forgive easily is a lack of transparency or preparation. Producing a realistic, fully costed budget signals to donors, lenders, and partners that your organization is capable, professional, and trustworthy.

The True Cost of Fundraising

When we talk about the cost of doing business, we often focus only on program expenses—the direct cost of delivering services. But for a nonprofit to thrive, we must also understand the cost of raising the money that makes those services possible.

Every fundraising activity has a true cost, even when it seems "free." Events, for example, are rarely as profitable as they appear. To understand their real return, we must count everything that goes into making them happen: staff hours, volunteer time, donated goods or services, marketing, setup, cleanup, and follow-up. In-kind and staff contributions are real costs; they simply don't appear on a traditional expense line.

If an event brings in $50,000 but requires 400 staff and volunteer hours, catering discounts, and marketing support worth another $20,000, the true cost wasn't zero—it was significant. Recognizing that full investment helps you assess whether the event was worth the effort and where improvements could be made next time.

Fundraising is part of your operations, not separate from it. Knowing what it truly costs to raise a dollar—whether through events, grants, or donor cultivation—builds financial clarity and credibility. It ensures that your organization prices its fundraising efforts realistically and makes informed decisions about where to invest time and resources for the greatest return.

Understanding these hidden costs doesn't discourage fundraising; it strengthens it. When you see the full picture, you can fundraise smarter, communicate your needs honestly to donors, and build a budget that reflects the real work it takes to sustain your mission.

Nonprofit Is a Tax Status, Not a Goal

Too many nonprofits believe that ending the year at zero is a sign of good stewardship. They're proud when every dollar is "put back into the mission" and the books balance perfectly. But this mindset, while well-intentioned, is one of the most dangerous myths in the sector.

A nonprofit's goal should never be to simply break even. That's not financial responsibility; it's financial fragility. Just as underbudgeting or undercharging for services leads to instability, failing to plan for a surplus limits an organization's ability to respond to crises, invest in innovation, or seize new opportunities.

A healthy nonprofit intentionally budgets for a surplus every year. That surplus isn't profit in the for-profit sense. Rather, it's reinvestment capital. It's what allows organizations to improve systems, invest in staff, strengthen programs, and fund the infrastructure that sustains impact over time. The truth is simple: a surplus is not greed; it offers capacity.

Surpluses are what make nonprofits resilient. They create breathing room, the flexibility to weather downturns, experiment with new ideas, and make strategic investments when opportunities arise. They also signal strength to funders. Donors and foundations are far more likely to invest in organizations that demonstrate fiscal discipline and a plan for long-term stability.

When an organization ends the year at zero, it means every dollar was spent, leaving no margin for the unexpected. Emergencies happen: a major grant falls through, a key staff member needs to be replaced, or a roof starts leaking. Without reserves or a surplus, even a small disruption can trigger layoffs, program cuts, or debt.

Without that cushion, sustainability quickly erodes. I've seen reimbursement rates so low that agencies lost hundreds of thousands of dollars each year just delivering contract services. An animal shelter that lost money every time it took in a stray because rising insurance and supply costs weren't built into their contract. The lesson is clear: know the true cost of your services, charge accordingly, and plan to earn more than you spend. Anything less is an invitation to crisis.

Building Reserves: Turning Surplus into Stability

A well-structured reserve fund ensures that surplus revenue strengthens the organization rather than sitting idle. Reserves function as the nonprofit's financial safety net, protecting against uncertainty, enabling innovation, and ensuring that short-term challenges don't derail long-term goals.

There are several types of reserves, each with a different purpose:

Operating Reserve—Covers general expenses during funding gaps or unexpected shortfalls.

Capital Reserve—Sets aside funds for major equipment purchases, facility repairs, or technology upgrades.

Opportunity Reserve—Provides flexible funds to pursue unexpected opportunities, such as launching a pilot program or matching a new grant.

Endowment Fund—Permanently invested capital where only the returns are used to support operations, ensuring long-term financial stability.

How much to keep in reserve depends on the organization's size, funding stability, and risk profile. Nonprofits with steady income might aim for three months of operating expenses, while those with fluctuating or seasonal funding should target six months or more in reserve. Organizations relying heavily on individual donations, large contracts, or program revenue benefit from maintaining a full year's reserves, offering protection from market or funding volatility.

To calculate the target reserve amount, review annual expenses and multiply the average monthly cost by the desired reserve period:

Average Monthly Expenses × Months of Reserve Desired = Reserve Goal

For example, if your organization spends $50,000 per month and aims for six months of reserves, the goal should be $300,000.

Managing and Replenishing Reserves

Once the target is set, establish clear policies for how reserves will be used, replenished, and reported. Specify under what conditions the funds may be accessed, such as emergencies, economic downturns, or cash flow disruptions, and how the organization will rebuild the balance afterward. Without defined rules, reserves can be depleted prematurely, undermining their purpose.

Start small and build gradually. Allocate 5–10% of annual revenue to reserves until the goal is met. Surpluses, unrestricted gifts, or windfall donations are excellent sources for initial funding. Some organizations also transfer excess operating funds to reserve accounts at the end of each fiscal year, with board approval.

Keep reserve funds in separate, low-risk accounts, such as money market funds or conservative mutual funds. The priority is liquidity and safety, not aggressive growth. A modest return that keeps pace with inflation is ideal, but reserves must remain accessible in times of need.

Restricted vs.Unrestricted Funds

One of the most important distinctions in nonprofit finance, and one of the most misunderstood, is the difference between restricted and unrestricted funds. Restricted funds are grants or donations that come with strings attached: they must be used for a specific purpose as defined by the donor. A foundation might award a $50,000 grant solely to support youth mentoring, or a corporate partner might fund only program materials. In these cases, the organization is both legally and ethically obligated to spend the money exactly as directed.

Unrestricted funds, by contrast, give the organization flexibility. These dollars can support what donors rarely see but every mission depends on: operating expenses, staff salaries, technology, rent, or fundraising activities.

While restricted funds are vital for program delivery, overreliance on them can mask financial instability. An organization may appear well-funded on paper yet still struggle to meet payroll or pay the rent because most of its income is locked into specific uses. This imbalance often leads to issues that quietly erode the organization's ability to deliver on its mission, such as deferred maintenance, underpaid staff, or underdeveloped infrastructure. Programs can only thrive when the systems behind them are strong.

Within the Five Factors™ framework, this dynamic directly links *Budget* to *Plan*. The strategic plan outlines what the organization intends to achieve; the budget must show how it will be funded. A sustainable financial plan includes not just the costs of programs but also the operational backbone that makes them possible. Relying too heavily on restricted dollars leaves that backbone fragile.

To build balance, nonprofits should proactively cultivate unrestricted support. This may include launching annual giving campaigns that emphasize the importance of keeping the lights on and staff employed or working with foundations that offer general operating grants. Building strong, trust-based relationships with donors also helps. When supporters understand the organization's overall impact and stewardship, they are more likely to give without restrictions.

Unrestricted funding essentially is capacity investment. It fuels innovation, resilience, and growth. The healthiest organizations maintain a mix of both restricted and unrestricted income, ensuring they can meet donor intent while sustaining the infrastructure required to deliver real, measurable impact.

Cash Flow Management

Even when a nonprofit has a balanced budget on paper, it may still struggle to pay its bills on time due to uneven timing of revenue and expenses. Many nonprofits receive large portions of their income at specific times of year, such as through an annual fundraising gala, a foundation grant that pays out once, or government reimbursements that are slow to arrive. Meanwhile, expenses like payroll, rent, and utilities come due every month. Without careful planning, these timing gaps can create periods of cash shortages, even when the organization is financially stable overall.

Effective cash flow management requires forecasting income and expenses on a monthly basis rather than relying solely on the annual budget. By projecting when funds will actually be received and when bills will come due, leaders can anticipate tight periods and prepare accordingly. Tools like cash flow calendars or rolling forecasts can provide visibility into these cycles.

Cash flow forecasting operates on a much more granular level, often monthly or even weekly. Nonprofits can use a simple spreadsheet or accounting software to map out projected grant disbursements, pledged donations, event revenue, and recurring contributions against known expenses such as payroll, rent, utilities, and program costs. By comparing inflows and outflows month by month, leadership can spot upcoming gaps before they become crises. For example, if a large grant is not scheduled to pay until October, but expenses remain steady through the summer, a forecast will highlight the shortfall months in advance, allowing the organization to prepare.

To bridge shortfalls, organizations typically rely on operating reserves, short-term lines of credit, or delayed expenses. Building a three- to six-month reserve is especially valuable, as it gives nonprofits the breathing room to weather delays in grant payments or fluctuations in donations without interrupting services. The strongest tool is a well-funded operating reserve, which are savings set aside specifically to cover timing issues or emergencies. However, when reserves are not yet established, some nonprofits turn to a line of credit with a bank or community lender. While borrowing introduces costs in the form of interest, a line of credit can provide stability during temporary cash shortages. Importantly, leaders should view these tools as bridges rather than solutions to structural deficits; they work best when paired with strong fundraising and financial management.

Monitoring Liquidity Month-to-Month

Forecasting and bridging strategies are only effective if cash flow is monitored consistently. This means tracking actual inflows and outflows against projections and updating the forecast regularly, ideally every month.

Key liquidity indicators, such as the current ratio (current assets divided by current liabilities) or the number of days cash on hand, are excellent starting points for assessing a nonprofit's financial health. These metrics help leaders understand whether the organization has the short-term resources needed to cover immediate obligations. A healthy current ratio (generally above 1.0) signals that the nonprofit can pay its bills, while days cash on hand provides a quick measure of how long the organization could continue operating if revenue were temporarily interrupted.

In addition to liquidity, there are other key indicators that the organization should regularly monitor:

- Operating surplus: This measures whether the organization is generating more than it uses or deficit from its operations. A positive operating surplus indicates sustainability and the ability to reinvest in programs, while a negative one may suggest the nonprofit is living beyond its means. It can be calculated through:
- Operating Surplus % = (Operating Revenue – Operating Expenses) ÷ Operating Revenue
- Revenue Diversity: Overreliance on a single funding source, such as one grant or one donor, creates risk. Analyzing the mix of funding streams (grants, donations, earned income, events, and contracts) shows whether the organization has a stable, diversified base to withstand changes in one area.
- Program Efficiency Ratio: This looks at how much of total spending goes directly to program services versus administrative or fundraising costs. While the "overhead myth" has been challenged, maintaining a healthy balance demonstrates that funds are being used effectively to achieve the mission.
- Debt-to-Asset Ratio: This ratio compares total liabilities to total assets and provides insight into how leveraged the organization is. A high ratio may indicate potential risk if too much of the nonprofit's resources are tied up in debt repayment. The ratio can be calculated as Debt-to-Asset Ratio = Total Liabilities/Total Assets
- Months of Liquid Cash: This is a simple way to describe financial resilience in nonprofit language. Itt tells you how many months your organization could keep operating if revenue slowed or paused, using only the unrestricted resources you can actually access. To calculate it, start with spendable, unrestricted dollars—cash and readily available reserves—and subtract anything that can't be used to pay bills now (such as buildings and equipment, endowment or long-term investments that aren't accessible, prepaid expenses, and other illiquid assets). Then divide that "liquid cash" by your average monthly operating expenses. The result is a clear, board-friendly number that helps leaders understand stability, prepare for seasonal funding cycles, and make decisions before a cash crunch becomes a crisis.

Taken together, these indicators provide a more holistic view of financial health. Liquidity ensures the organization can meet immediate obligations, operating margins reveal whether it is living within its means, and diversity, efficiency, and reserves highlight long-term sustainability.

Regularly reviewing these measures empowers boards and staff to make informed decisions and address risks before they become crises. Ideally, they should be reviewed quarterly to ensure the organization is operating well, allows for adjustments to be made quickly before the organization goes off-track, and builds a culture of proactive financial stewardship. For example, if monthly monitoring shows that accounts receivable are consistently lagging, leadership can work with funders or donors to adjust payment schedules. By institutionalizing cash flow monitoring, nonprofits gain the agility to make timely adjustments and avoid the kind of last-minute scrambling that damages trust with staff, vendors, and funders.

Gauging the Financial Health of Your Organization

The following form was adapted from commonly seen questions coming from government and foundation compliance. We've adapted it here so that you can gain a measure of where your organization is and pinpoint areas where the fiscal health can be strengthened:

Fiscal Questionnaire	*Response*
Organization Name:	
Completed By (Name, Title):	
Date:	
I. Organizational Data	
Name of Accounting System:	
Total Agency Federal Awards:	
Total Agency State Awards:	
Does your organization have internal control policies/ procedures?	
If yes, date of last review.	
Start date for Fiscal Year:	
II. Financial Statement/Independent Audit	
Date of last audit or financial statement review:	
Name of Audit Agency/Firm:	

(*Continued*)

Fiscal Questionnaire	*Response*
Was the opinion unmodified?	
If modified, state reason.	
Date submitted to Single Audit Unit and Contract Manager:	
Were findings reported?	
If yes, please explain.	
If yes, what was the agency's response(s) to the finding(s), and in what time frame were corrective actions to be completed?	
Date of the last filing of IRS 990 or 990EZ.	
III. Board of Directors	
Does the Board of Directors have a Finance Committee?	
How frequently does the Finance Committee meet? For what purpose(s)?	
What financial documents/reports are provided to the Board of Directors?	
How often?	
Presented by whom?	
How far in advance of meetings are the financials provided? If applicable, are the financial reports presented to the Finance Committee prior to the regular board meeting?	
What is the process for the financial statements to be reviewed as a board? (Reviewed first by/with the Finance Committee?)	
How often does the Board receive training on reading and analyzing financial statements?	
When was the last time the Board received training on reading and analyzing financial statements?	
Presented by whom?	
IV. Fundraising	

(*Continued*)

Fiscal Questionnaire	*Response*
Please explain your organization's fundraising events/ efforts for this fiscal year.	
Is there anything in particular the organization is fundraising for (any special projects or improvements)?	
If yes, please explain.	
What is the projected income from each event/ effort?	
Is your solicitation license up to date and active?	
Does your organization currently use services from a fund raising consultant?	
If yes, have their appropriate licenses and required filings been verified?	
V. Travel	
What is your organization's policy on CEO/ED and staff travel (approval, reimbursement, and check signing)?	
VI. Cash Flow	
Does your organization have a cash flow projection statement?	
If yes, who prepares it?	
If yes, who reviews? How often?	
If not, what is your policy on cash flow? How are you managing it?	
Do you have concerns with the organization's cash flow?	
If yes, what steps are you taking to address the concerns?	
Does your organization have reserves?	
If yes, please describe?	
If not, how would you manage a financial crisis?	

(Continued)

Fiscal Questionnaire	*Response*
How many months of expenses can your organization currently cover should there be an extended interruption in federal and/or state funding?	
At what point would the organization have to reduce programs or staffing? If that happened, what would it look like?	
Does the organization have a written plan in place in the event this should occur? Who has access to and input into the plan? How often is it reviewed and updated?	
How often are you overspending on budgeted line items?	
If you are, why is that occurring and how is it being addressed?	
If you have, did the overspending meet the requirements to be presented to the board?	
VIII. Invoicing	
How do you ensure that you are not double-billing?	
Has your organization requested expedited payment to meet any financial obligation(s)?	
If yes, when was the request and why?	
Was the request approved?	
If not, what action(s) was taken to fulfill the financial obligation(s)?	
VIII. Line of Credit	
Does your organization have a line of credit?	
If yes, how many?	
If yes, the amount of credit?	
If yes, what is the available balance?	
If yes, what is your organization's general plan to repay?	
If yes, how does your organization secure the loan?	

(*Continued*)

Fiscal Questionnaire	*Response*
IX. Match	
What are your sources of match?	
How do you ensure you are not charging a match to more than one funding source?	
How do you reconcile all match requirements?	
How often do you reconcile matches?	
If errors were found, how would they be corrected? Please list all steps.	
X. Banking	
How many bank accounts does the organization maintain?	
Name of financial institutions of current bank accounts:	

Transparency to Build Trust Internally and Externally

Believe it or not, creating a strong budget and accounting system can be translated into fundraising. Proper accounting practices do far more than satisfy auditors or meet compliance requirements, they can become powerful tools for storytelling and trust-building. When a nonprofit maintains accurate, transparent financial records, it gains access to valuable data that helps explain how resources are used and what impact they create. This kind of clarity is exactly what potential donors look for when deciding where to invest their money. They want assurance that the organization understands its finances, allocates funds responsibly, and demonstrates real results.

Transparency is most effective when it is clear, consistent, and accessible. One of the simplest ways to achieve this is by creating a donor-friendly annual report that combines financial information with programmatic outcomes. Rather than presenting only tables of numbers, nonprofits can show charts or graphs that illustrate how funds are allocated across programs, administrative costs, and fundraising. Highlighting specific successes, such as the number of clients served or measurable improvements in community outcomes, connects financial stewardship to real-world impact. Including a message from the executive director or board chair can further contextualize the organization's financial story and reinforce accountability.

Another key step is making IRS Form 990 available in a way that is easy for donors to understand. While the 990 is a legal document, it can be overwhelming for people unfamiliar with nonprofit accounting. Summarizing the key sections, such as revenue sources, program expenses, administrative costs, and executive compensation, to make the information digestible while preserving transparency. Posting both the full IRS 990 form and a plain-language summary on the organization's website ensures accessibility and signals openness.

Nonprofits can also proactively communicate financial updates throughout the year, not just at year-end. Quarterly newsletters, donor emails, or social media updates about fundraising progress and expenditures reinforce the organization's commitment to accountability. This regular communication helps donors see how their contributions are being used in real time, creating trust and reinforcing engagement.

Finally, leveraging third-party rating organizations such as Charity Navigator, GuideStar or Candid can add an extra layer of credibility. Nonprofits should ensure their profiles are complete, accurate, and up to date, including recent audits, governance policies, and performance metrics. Highlighting high ratings or seals of approval on websites and in donor communications can reassure supporters that the organization meets rigorous standards for financial health and transparency. Together, these practices create a culture of openness, foster donor confidence, and ultimately strengthen the organization's ability to attract and retain long-term support.

Leveraging Technology for Financial Strength and Impact

Technology now sits at the heart of how nonprofits operate, connect, and grow. The right systems can transform how an organization raises funds, manages donor relationships, tracks outcomes, and ensures accountability. Yet many nonprofits struggle to select tools that truly fit their size, mission, and capacity. It's common to see organizations adopt software because it's popular, recommended by peers, or free, only to discover that it doesn't integrate with existing systems or staff workflows. The key to choosing the right technology is clarity: understanding what your organization *really needs* to achieve its goals.

That may mean implementing a customer relationship management (CRM) platform, accounting software, data visualization tools, or all three. The goal isn't simply to have technology in place; it's to ensure these tools actively enhance efficiency, deepen impact, and help leaders make informed, mission-aligned decisions. Every technology investment should connect directly to the strategic plan and support long-term sustainability.

Nonprofits benefit most when financial and relationship management systems work together. Customer relationship management (CRM) and donor management tools enhance fiscal oversight by linking fundraising activity directly to organizational operations. They track donor contributions, pledges, and interactions, revealing giving trends and helping staff forecast revenue with greater accuracy.

When CRMs and accounting platforms integrate, they provide a unified financial picture, showing not only what funds are raised but also how they are spent. This integration prevents mismanagement of restricted versus unrestricted funds and supports compliance with donor and grant requirements. It also allows leadership to see how fundraising performance directly affects program capacity and impact, aligning financial management with mission outcomes.

Accounting Software: The Foundation of Financial Health

Strong accounting systems form the backbone of sound financial operations. They automate routine but essential tasks: expense tracking, payroll, invoicing, and reporting, freeing staff to focus on strategy instead of spreadsheets. Automation minimizes errors and increases efficiency, while real-time reporting gives leadership accurate, up-to-date insight into revenue, expenses, and cash flow.

These platforms make financial transparency actionable. With accurate data at their fingertips, executives and boards can quickly assess the organization's fiscal health and adjust as needed. As discussed throughout this framework, regular financial check-ins are essential to sustainability, and accounting software provides the continuous visibility needed to manage proactively rather than reactively.

When configured properly, technology also strengthens internal controls and reduces financial risk. Most modern accounting systems can require approval workflows for expenses, flag irregular transactions, and maintain complete audit trails. Automated reporting reduces opportunities for human error or misreporting, while digital records simplify compliance with grant and regulatory requirements.

Cloud-based platforms add another layer of value by improving both accessibility and security. Board members, finance committees, and auditors can review financial information remotely without compromising sensitive data. This accessibility ensures transparency while maintaining control, creating an environment of trust and accountability across all levels of governance.

Turning Data into Strategic Insight

Beyond compliance, the greatest value of technology lies in its ability to transform data into insight. Dashboards and analytics tools give nonprofit leaders the ability to visualize trends, compare program costs and returns, and model the impact of future decisions before implementing them. These tools turn financial data into strategy, helping leaders test scenarios, allocate resources effectively, and communicate clearly with donors about cost, outcomes, and impact.

Integrated systems ultimately strengthen every element of the Five Factors™ Framework:

- Plan: Data-driven forecasting links strategy to realistic costs and outcomes.
- Outcomes: Measurable metrics show program performance and ROI.
- Budget: Real-time visibility enables responsible, responsive financial management.
- Team: Efficiency tools free staff to focus on mission-critical work.
- Donors: Transparent reporting builds trust and long-term investment.

By aligning technology with mission, nonprofits can use it to guide strategy, build accountability, and sustain growth. When financial and program systems work in harmony, organizations gain not just operational efficiency but also the clarity and credibility needed to thrive.

Getting the Board on Board

There are few moments more daunting for an executive than walking into a board meeting with a carefully prepared budget, only to hear that it's "too ambitious." Too often, boards respond to projected fundraising gaps by demanding cuts instead of solutions. In the name of fiscal caution, organizations slash programs, freeze wages, or defer maintenance, all decisions that look responsible on paper but quietly erode the organization's capacity to function.

The instinct to reduce the budget at all costs can backfire. Shrinking a budget to reach zero does not make an organization healthier; it simply hides the true cost of doing business. If you budget front-desk wages at $15 an hour when the going market rate is $25, those positions will remain unfilled. Operations stall, staff morale dips, and service quality suffers. Understated budgets eventually result in burnout, turnover, and missed opportunities. Worse, they create mistrust, both internally, when staff see unrealistic numbers, and externally, when funders sense instability.

Linking Financial Realities to the Strategic Plan

In the Five Factors™ Framework, the Budget is not just a financial document; it is a manifestation of the Plan. Every strategic goal has a cost, and every cost needs to be supported by a realistic funding strategy. A board that insists on approving only "balanced" budgets without understanding the investment required to achieve growth is unintentionally holding the organization back.

A strong plan identifies both the expenses and the resources needed to achieve measurable outcomes. It outlines not only how much an initiative will cost but also how it will be funded (grants, earned income, corporate partnerships, or individual giving). This transparency gives board members confidence that the leadership team has thought through the trade-offs and contingencies and reassures donors that the organization has a roadmap grounded in both vision and fiscal responsibility.

Boards often hesitate to approve multi-year "growth budgets," fearing that staff will not be able to raise the necessary funds. The solution is education and partnership, not retreat. Bring in volunteer financial experts, CPAs, or consultants to help unpack cost drivers and market rates. Show how the budget ties to measurable outcomes, reserve policies, and risk management strategies. When board members understand how investments translate into impact and how much it costs to replace talent, update systems, or sustain growth, they are far more likely to support ambitious plans.

Financial Literacy as a Governance Imperative

Board effectiveness depends on financial literacy. Every member, regardless of background, should understand how to read a budget, a balance sheet, and a cash flow report. Without this knowledge, boards cannot exercise true oversight. They may approve budgets without realizing the implications of deferred maintenance, rising insurance premiums, or underfunded positions.

Financially literate boards ask better questions. They can spot trends, identify red flags early, and partner with staff to solve problems before they escalate. They understand not only where the money is going but also *why* and how those expenses align with the organization's mission and strategic goals.

To build this competency, integrate financial education into every stage of board service. Offer onboarding sessions for new members that include a primer on nonprofit financial statements and key ratios. Schedule short workshops or refreshers throughout the year tied to the finance calendar, before audit season, during budget review, or following major grants. Consider inviting external experts to present on emerging financial issues, such as inflationary pressures or changes in accounting standards for nonprofits.

The Finance Committee as a Strategic Partner

A strong Finance Committee transforms financial management from a perfunctory review into a strategic function. This committee, ideally composed of members with financial expertise, should meet regularly with the executive and accounting teams to review budget drafts, monitor cash flow, and interpret financial reports. They act as a bridge, translating financial realities for the full board and ensuring leadership is operating within sound policies.

Beyond basic oversight, a proactive Finance Committee can lead initiatives like establishing reserve funds, developing investment policies, or reviewing risk management practices. They can also ensure compliance with audit requirements and recommend steps to strengthen internal controls. By engaging in these activities, the committee not only supports the executive team but also reinforces the board's fiduciary duty to protect the organization's assets.

For smaller nonprofits, replicating a full committee structure may not be realistic, but that doesn't mean financial oversight can be ignored. Even a single board member with a background in accounting or business can serve as a "financial liaison," reviewing monthly reports and providing summaries for the group. This approach keeps the board informed without overwhelming staff or volunteers.

Scaled Financial Oversight for Small Nonprofits

Financial transparency and literacy are not luxuries reserved for large organizations. They are just as vital for small nonprofits, perhaps even more so. When staff and board members wear multiple hats, every financial decision carries significant weight. But smaller organizations can scale their approach to match their capacity.

- **Focus on Key Metrics**
  Boards don't need to wade through 20-page financial packets to be effective. A simple one-page summary can convey essential information: current cash balance, monthly revenue and expenses, grant pipeline, and outstanding payables. When presented clearly, these indicators give board members the insight to spot patterns, such as if donations are slowing, costs are creeping up, or reserves are dwindling.
- **Train Efficiently**
  Even organizations with limited budgets can support financial learning. Free webinars from state nonprofit associations, written guides, or brief tutorials during meetings can build foundational understanding. Encourage board members to ask questions. Financial literacy grows through dialogue, not silence.
- **Use Accessible Tools**
  Nonprofit-friendly platforms can automatically generate financial reports that align with standard accounting principles. Local nonprofit support centers, the IRS, and platforms such as Candid, Charity

Navigator, and GuideStar offer templates, examples, and training materials to help strengthen internal capacity.

- **Simplify the Structure**
  If the organization lacks enough members for a formal Finance Committee, delegate financial review to a small working group or a single financial liaison. That person can meet with staff monthly, review statements, and provide a high-level summary at each board meeting. This keeps financial discussions active and ensures accountability without overcomplicating governance.
- **Recruit for Financial Expertise**
  Every nonprofit benefits from having at least one board member with financial acumen, whether a CPA, banker, or business owner. When recruiting new members, make financial literacy part of the criteria. These individuals not only bring valuable oversight skills but can mentor other members and strengthen donor confidence.

Summary—Money Tells the Mission's Story

Even the most well-funded and mission-driven nonprofits can fall into financial traps; operating from fear instead of foresight, underpricing their services, or treating "breaking even" as success. These missteps often stem from habit, inexperience, or outdated beliefs about what it means to be a nonprofit. As this chapter illustrates, financial sustainability is about strategy, not austerity.

Financial clarity touches every part of the Five Factors™ Framework:

- Plan: Every goal should include a budget line that defines cost and funding source.
- Outcomes: Measure not only results but the cost per outcome. What does each unit of change cost to achieve?
- Team: Ensure competitive compensation and financial support for professional growth to retain talent.
- Donors: Share financials openly to demonstrate efficiency, credibility, and readiness for investment.

A strong fiscal plan does more than balance a budget. It provides a roadmap for how the organization will grow, adapt, and fulfill its mission over time. Financial leadership means knowing the true cost of programs, paying fair market rates, budgeting for a surplus, and building reserves that safeguard both mission and momentum. It's the difference between surviving year to year and leading with confidence across decades.

Too many organizations fall into the trap of fear-based budgeting and resort to cutting expenses, deferring investments, or shrinking their ambitions to avoid risk. But playing small doesn't protect a nonprofit; it weakens it. The antidote is strategic budgeting: making informed, data-driven decisions that balance responsibility with courage. By linking financial planning directly to outcomes and strategic goals, nonprofits can invest wisely, innovate freely, and grow sustainably.

Another common pitfall is underestimating true costs in service delivery, salaries, or capital projects. Nonprofits must calculate the real cost per unit of service, allocate shared expenses across programs, and ensure fees, reimbursements, or grants actually cover expenses. The same rigor applies to construction and infrastructure investments: every budget should include accurate market estimates and contingency funds (typically 10–20%) to prevent mid-project shortfalls that erode donor trust.

Financial health also depends on paying market rate for labor and services. Underpaying staff may save money in the short term, but it leads to burnout, turnover, and inefficiency in the long run. Competitive wages, fair benefits, and professional development investments are capacity-building strategies that strengthen the entire organization.

Equally important is recognizing that nonprofit is a tax status, not a goal. A healthy organization budgets for a surplus, not zero. That surplus becomes the foundation for building reserves: operating, capital, and opportunity funds that allow nonprofits to weather downturns, respond to emergencies, and seize new opportunities without jeopardizing operations. By setting aside even 5–10% of annual revenue, organizations create a financial safety net that ensures flexibility and long-term stability.

Finally, nonprofits must think beyond the fiscal year. A one-year budget answers the question, "Can we get through this year?" Multi-year financial plans (typically for three to five years) ask, "How do we grow our impact over time?" Long-term planning allows for diversification of revenue streams, proactive investment in infrastructure, and alignment with the organization's broader strategic goals.

Transparency must extend both inward and outward. Internally, it builds alignment between staff and board. Externally, it signals credibility to funders and the public. Post your audited statements, IRS Form 990, and concise budget summaries on your website. Include plain-language explanations of key figures, such as what portion of revenue supports programs, administration, and fundraising, and frame these numbers in the context of outcomes and impact, not just expense ratios.

Financial stewardship is a shared responsibility. Executives provide the data; accountants interpret it; boards ensure it aligns with mission and strategy. When all three work together, with realistic budgets, transparent reporting, and clear financial education, the organization earns something money can't buy: trust.

Key Takeaways

- A strong fiscal plan is a multi-year roadmap that connects financial decisions to mission outcomes.
- Fear-based budgeting limits growth; strategic budgeting empowers it.
- Know and price the true cost of every program, including fair wages and market-rate expenses.
- Always include contingency funds for capital projects and major initiatives.
- Budget for a surplus. Zero is not the goal. Surpluses fuel reserves and innovation.
- Maintain at least three to six months of operating reserves, with clear policies for use and replenishment.
- Diversify revenue streams to reduce dependence on any single source.
- Review financial performance regularly and adjust as needed to stay on course.

Progress Check

After reading this chapter, rate where your organization is on a scale of one to five, with one being that your organization does not have this component, or is just beginning to work on it, and five being that your organization is fully operational and has this element ready for vetting by a major donor.

Notes:

Chapter 3

Why Outcomes Matter

The Proof Behind the Purpose

Just as strong financial management builds credibility, strong outcome measurement builds trust. Donors want proof, and clients deserve results.

Years ago, during a board meeting, I posed a simple question to each member: "What keeps you up at night?" Most responses were predictable: finances, media, and staffing. However, one board member paused, surveyed the room, and quietly stated, "I worry we aren't making it stop." A profound silence fell upon the room. We all understood her meaning. We were tirelessly raising funds, running programs, and serving people, yet we questioned whether our efforts were truly creating a long-term solution to end the violence. Were we solving the problem, or merely managing it?

That moment changed how I thought about nonprofit success. It isn't enough to have passion, purpose, and programs. Donors, funders, and, most importantly, the people we serve deserve to know whether our work is making a measurable difference. After all, when someone trusts their life to you when you say you can keep them safe or help them get a job to feed their family, we need to know we can and do deliver.

To show evidence of success and the ability to fulfill their mission, organizations must demonstrate what outcomes they have produced. How many families found stable housing? How many children improved in school? How many pets were adopted into permanent homes and stayed there?

Outputs, like the number of shelter nights, hotline calls, or counseling sessions, are easy to track and satisfy most grants. But they only tell part of the story. Outcomes capture the lasting change those services create: how many survivors achieved long-term safety, how many participants found jobs that pay a living wage, or how many families moved from crisis to stability.

One national study found that 71% of nonprofits struggle to measure outcomes effectively. The lesson is clear: without demonstrating deeper, measurable impact, organizations risk leaving major funding opportunities on the table. Donors, especially those capable of transformational gifts,

DOI: 10.4324/9781003746218-4

want proof that their investment drives meaningful and lasting change. Even worse, they risk offering services that don't help, or even hurt.

One of the most important shifts nonprofits must make is moving from reporting outputs to reporting outcomes. Donors consistently say they want evidence of impact and ROI, yet most organizations still frame their work in terms of activity. The result? They unintentionally undersell their value.

The difference is more than semantics. Studies show that donors respond with *larger gifts* when they see outcomes expressed as return on investment, or ROI. A counseling session, for example, isn't just an hour of staff time. Rather, it represents public dollars saved in emergency mental health response, healthcare, and criminal justice costs. When nonprofits can demonstrate that every dollar invested yields multiple dollars in community benefit, they transform the donor's mindset from *charitable gift* to *smart investment*. That shift builds confidence, expands reach, and makes the case that philanthropy isn't just about generosity but also measurable return.

> Outputs vs. Outcomes—How to Tell Them Apart
>
> **Outputs** = activities (what we do)
> **Outcomes** = change (what happens because we did it).
> Most nonprofits confuse effort with effect. Donors no longer do.

The Role of Outcomes in the Five Factors™ Framework

In the Five Factors™ Framework, *Outcomes* serve as the connective tissue. Impact translates a nonprofit's *Plan* into measurable results, validates how the *Budget* is used, confirms the *Team's* effectiveness, and strengthens the case for *Donor* investment. Without outcomes, the entire structure wobbles because there's no proof that the work is achieving what it set out to do.

Each of the Five Factors™ depends on outcomes:

- **Plan:** Defines what success looks like.
- **Budget:** Demonstrates efficient and effective resource use.
- **Team:** Creates accountability and shared ownership.
- **Donors:** Builds confidence that their support drives measurable change.

Outcome measurement is the thread that ties all Five Factors™ together.

Understanding the Continuum: From Inputs to ROI

Every nonprofit collects numbers, but not every number tells the story donors want to hear. Most organizations proudly report how many meals they served, classes they taught, or clients they reached. Counting what's easy to measure is tempting. Outputs like the number of students assisted, pounds of pet food given away, or, or books read are visible, required by most grants, and look impressive in graphic form. But they don't prove that lives improved or problems diminished; they only tell *part* of the story. What donors, policymakers, and communities truly want to understand is what *changed* because of those activities.

Donors respond to clarity. They want concise, accessible language that cuts through complexity. Imagine the power of saying, "We reduced gun violence in our city by 80%," or "Seventy-six percent of traumatic brain injury survivors we served regained independent living." These statements are direct, data-driven, and emotionally resonant. They demonstrate that your work is effective.

Institutional funders, from foundations to government agencies, increasingly require this kind of proof. They expect evidence of impact as a condition of grantmaking. Nonprofits with robust outcome systems, namely those that can show measurable progress and ROI, stand out in competitive funding environments and gain access to new revenue streams across local, state, and federal levels.

Outcome reporting articulates where the organization is going and how it plans to get there. When a nonprofit can say with confidence, "Here's what we set out to do, here's what we achieved, and here's how we'll build on it," it moves beyond good intentions and into the realm of measurable impact, the kind donors, funders, and communities can believe in.

To get there, we have to understand the full continuum of impact, which moves through four connected stages:

The Four Levels of Outcome Measurement

Level	*Definition*	*Key Question*	*Example*
Input	The **resources or participants** that go *into* an activity—time, funding, staff, or number of people who begin a service or program. Inputs reflect your organization's *effort* and capacity.	What are we investing or who is participating?	250 people enroll in the job-readiness course.

(Continued)

Level	*Definition*	*Key Question*	*Example*
Output	The **direct activities or completions** that result from those inputs. Outputs show what your organization *did*—the tangible products or services delivered.	What did we do or deliver?	180 participants completed all training modules.
Outcome	The **measurable change** that occurred *because of* the program. Outcomes reflect the difference your activity made in people's lives, behaviors, or circumstances.	What changed for participants as a result?	120 graduates obtained full-time jobs with higher wages within six months.
Return on investment (ROI)	The **economic or social value** created by those outcomes—including cost savings, avoided expenses, or broader community benefits. ROI translates human progress into financial impact.	Why does this change matter to the community or economy?	The community saves $500,000 annually in public assistance costs and gains $1.2 million in new taxable income.

Why the Full Continuum Matters

Organizations that stop at counting inputs and outputs sell themselves short. They appear busy instead of effective and compassionate instead of strategic. Donors often interpret output-heavy reporting as a lack of sophistication or evidence of limited impact.

By contrast, organizations that measure and communicate outcomes and ROI tell a far more powerful story. They:

- Attract larger, multi-year grants and corporate partnerships.
- Command greater credibility with policymakers and media.
- Build stronger donor loyalty through proof of effectiveness.

Mastering the full continuum, from inputs to ROI, redefines an organization's identity. It elevates nonprofits from *helpers* to *problem solvers*. They move from *doing good work* to *proving good works*. And in doing so, they earn the trust, investment, and influence required to scale real change.

Relationship between Outcomes and Gift Size

Every nonprofit has a story to tell, but not all evidence carries the same weight with donors and funders. Think of each level of measurement as a tool in your toolkit. Each data point, whether it's a client story, demographic information, or an economic ROI, reveals part of your organization's impact. Used together, these tools create a complete narrative of change.

As you move up the hierarchy of evidence, the level of credibility, sophistication, and donor confidence increases. Most nonprofits report only inputs and outputs, stopping at what they did rather than what changed. That's like describing the ingredients of a meal and how many plates were served, but never saying whether anyone was nourished. Inputs and outputs show *effort*; outcomes and ROI prove *effectiveness*.

When a nonprofit only talks about the number of people served, it sounds active but not necessarily impactful. Donors may appreciate the dedication yet still wonder: *Are we actually solving the problem?* Counting what you did, without showing what changed, leaves that question, and your funding, unanswered.

Many organizations are taught that an inspiring story alone can secure a major gift. While stories are essential for emotional connection, transformational donors need more. They want proof that emotion translates into measurable impact. The following diagram illustrates how to combine stories, outputs, outcomes, and ROI to move donors from compassion to confidence, building both trust and investment. The higher you climb, the stronger and more compelling your case becomes.

The Nonprofit Storytelling Spectrum—From Emotion to Evidence

Telling your story is essential, but storytelling alone is not enough. The most successful nonprofits understand that communication with donors evolves along a spectrum, from emotional connection to measurable ROI. Each stage appeals to different motivations and requires different tools (Figure 3.1).

At the foundation of this Nonprofit Toolkit for Impact Communication are stories, the personal, emotional narratives that draw donors into your mission. Stories of lives changed, families strengthened, and communities transformed are powerful entry points. They inspire empathy and action, particularly among annual donors who give because they feel connected to the cause.

Moving upward, we introduce inputs and demographics: data showing who you serve, how you serve them, and where your programs reach. This

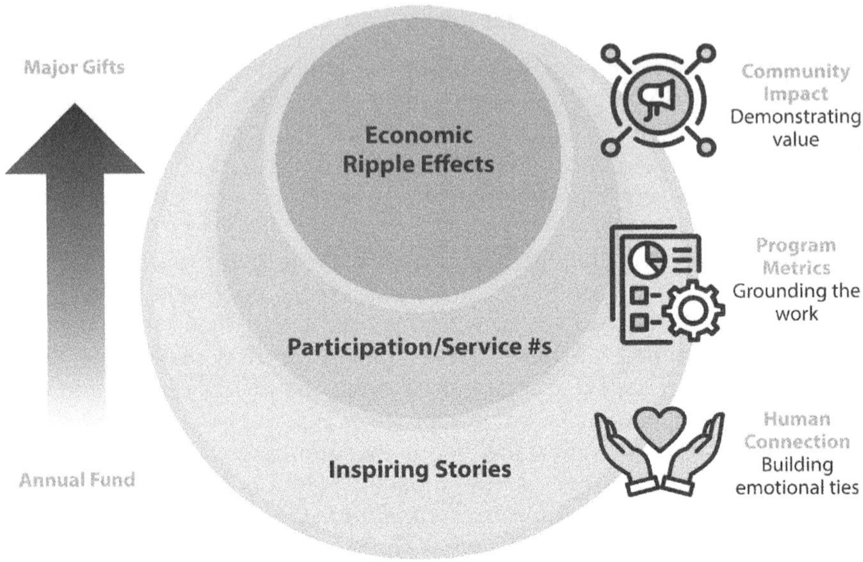

Figure 3.1 Consider the larger implications of your organization's work on a community scale. This in combination with inspiring stories and other metrics offers a more robust depiction.

layer builds credibility and demonstrates scale, showing mid-level donors and institutional funders that your work is not anecdotal but systematic and inclusive.

Next come the outputs: the tangible results of your efforts. These are the numbers that prove progress: meals served, children tutored, shelters opened, and jobs created. Outputs provide assurance that donations translate into measurable activity and operational efficiency.

At the top of the spectrum lies impact and ROI, the highest level of proof. Here, the story evolves from "what we did" to "what changed because of what we did." Donors at this level, those considering major or transformational gifts, are motivated by both emotion and evidence. They invest because they trust that their contributions generate measurable, lasting change.

This is where the Five Factors™ Framework converges: clear plans, strong outcomes, sound budgets, aligned teams, and engaged donors come together to show that your organization is ready for large-scale investment.

Every layer of the spectrum matters.

Stories ignite passion.

Data builds trust.

Impact sustains investment.

1 **Stories—Emotional Connection**
Individual narratives that humanize the mission.
Example: "Maria found safety and stability after leaving an abusive relationship."
Used for: annual giving, awareness, social media.
2 **Outputs—Activity Measures**
What your organization does.
Example: "We provided 12,000 shelter nights last year."
Used for: operational reporting, grant compliance.
3 **Outcomes—Change Measures**
How lives or systems improved because of your work.
Example: "84% of participants secured permanent housing within six months."
Used for: donor cultivation, case for support, and ROI calculations.
4 **Impact/ROI—Systemic Results and Return**
The long-term transformation and economic value generated.
Example: "Every $1 invested saves $4 in public costs."
Used for: major gifts, multi-year funding, and policy advocacy.

The Higher You Climb, the More Compelling Your Story Becomes

The higher you climb on the hierarchy of evidence, the more credible and fundable your story becomes. Stories open hearts; outcomes and ROI open doors to transformational investment.

Consider a domestic violence shelter that proudly reports it provided 12,000 nights of safety last year. That statistic shows the organization was active, but not necessarily effective. It tells us the team worked hard, not whether families left safer, more stable, or self-sufficient.

Now imagine instead reporting:

> Eighty-four percent of survivors secured permanent housing within six months, reducing community costs by $18 million annually.

That single shift moves the narrative from *We did a lot* to *We made a measurable difference*. Donors see not just compassion but competence and a clear ROI.

Economic framing doesn't replace empathy; it amplifies it. When nonprofits demonstrate how social problems ripple through healthcare systems, workplaces, and public budgets, they reveal that these aren't isolated personal struggles but rather costly, community-wide challenges that affect everyone.

The following chart illustrates how each level of evidence communicates impact in different ways and for different purposes. Together, they form a complete narrative of transformation that strengthens donor confidence and elevates investment potential.

Level	*Definition*	*Example*	*Best Used for*
Stories	Human stories that inspire emotion and connection.	"Tanya rebuilt her life through our program."	Annual fund appeals, awareness campaigns.
Outputs	Activities and services delivered.	5,200 meals served, 220 students tutored.	Grant reporting, operations summaries.
Outcomes	Changes that result from outputs.	80% of students improved reading levels.	Donor cultivation, mid-level asks, dashboards.
Impact/ ROI	Long-term transformation and measurable ROI.	$1 invested yields $5 in community value.	Major gifts, endowments, partnerships.

This integrated approach gives donors and funders both the heart and the head they need to confidently say *yes*. It humanizes data, strengthens credibility, and turns goodwill into sustained investment.

Funders, corporate partners, and policymakers must often justify their commitments to boards or taxpayers. By presenting both emotional stories and credible financial data, nonprofits give them the dual rationale they need, compassion and logic working in tandem. Each level builds credibility, moving the story from activity to accountability to value. The higher you go, the stronger your case for investment becomes.

Putting It into Practice: Beginning Your Outcome Measurement Journey

Outcome measurement is simply about defining what success looks like and then checking to see if you're getting there. Think of it as taking inventory of your organization's story. Every program, service, and initiative you offer has inputs (what goes in), outputs (what you do), outcomes (what changes), and ROI (the value those changes create for individuals and communities).

To begin, gather your team and build a program data inventory. This doesn't have to be complicated. Open a spreadsheet, whiteboard, or large sheet of paper and list every program or service your organization offers. Next to each one, write down:

Who it serves: Who are the primary beneficiaries? Are there indirect beneficiaries as well (families, employers, schools, the community)?

What it provides: What services, supports, or opportunities does the program deliver? Be specific: counseling hours, meals, tutoring sessions, workshops, case management, etc.

What you think happens as a result: What do you believe changes because of this work? Do families find stability? Do youth graduate? Do animals find permanent homes?

You've just taken the first step in creating an outcome map. Now it's time to bring that insight to life.

Use these questions to capture a clear picture of what each of your programs does, who it serves, and how you measure its effectiveness. Complete one page per program or service. Start with what you know, then identify where information is missing and what you'll need to fill the gaps.

This tool helps you see where data already exists, where it needs to be strengthened, and how each program contributes to your overall impact. Over time, these findings will sharpen your outcome measurement, improve communication with donors, and create a stronger, more confident narrative of change.

How to Use This Template

1 **List every program or service.**
Include both direct services, such as food distribution, counseling, or training, and indirect activities like advocacy, outreach, or community education. This ensures you capture the full scope of your organization's work.

2 **Describe who the program serves and what it provides.**
Be specific about age groups, demographics, or target populations, and briefly describe the core support or services offered.

3 **Identify inputs, outputs, and outcomes.**

- **Inputs** are resources or activities that go into the program, such as the number of participants enrolled, hotline calls answered, or client intakes completed.
- **Outputs** are what you produce or deliver, the classes held, meals served, or clients counseled.
- **Outcomes** are the real-world changes that occur as a result: families achieving stability, youth graduating, and animals adopted into permanent homes.

4 **Estimate ROI or broader economic value.**
Consider the return your program generates: financial, social, or community-wide. If exact numbers aren't available, use reasonable proxies such as "reduced emergency room visits," "increased tax contributions," or "improved graduation rates." We will explain how to do this later in the chapter.

5 **Audit your data sources.**
Identify where your information currently lives, in client management systems, grant reports, surveys, or external databases, and mark what's missing or incomplete.

6 **Create a plan.**
Outline practical next steps: what data needs to be collected, who is responsible, and how often it will be reviewed. Over time, this process becomes the foundation of your program evaluation cycle, ensuring your organization continuously learns, adapts, and improves.

Program Data Inventory Template

Program/Service Name

(*Write the program or initiative name here.*)

Who It Serves

- Primary participants or clients: Secondary or indirect beneficiaries (families, employers, community):

What It Provides

Describe the key activities or services offered (e.g., job training, counseling, housing, after-school tutoring).

Inputs (Resources Invested)

List the people, time, materials, and funding required to run this program.

Examples: 2 staff members, 40 volunteer hours per month, and $25,000 in supplies and grants.

Outputs (What's Delivered)

Record tangible counts of activity.

Examples: 120 classes taught, 75 clients served, and 4 community workshops.

Outcomes (What Changes as a Result)

Define the measurable change that happens for participants.

Examples: 85% gained employment within 6 months, 70% increased reading levels, and 60% maintained stable housing for a year.

ROI/Economic Value

Estimate the broader ROI or community value.

Examples: $420,000 in new wages earned, $90,000 in avoided emergency-care costs, and $4 in impact for every $1 invested.

Existing Data Sources

Identify where current information lives—surveys, databases, partner reports, public data, etc.

Data Gaps/Needs

Note what's missing or unclear.

Examples: No post-program surveys, incomplete demographic data, or need for partner follow-up.

Next Steps/Evaluation Plan

Outline concrete actions to strengthen measurement.

Examples: Add exit surveys, share data with partners quarterly, and schedule an annual program review.

Keep completed sheets together as your organization's data inventory file. Review and update them annually to track progress and refine your evaluation process. Ask yourself,

- Does existing data confirm the program's effectiveness?
- What additional evidence or research could strengthen your case?
- How can these results be shared with donors or community partners?

If you discover gaps, don't be discouraged, as this is where the most meaningful progress begins. Donors value organizations that are honest about what they know *and* what they're learning. You can even include this process in donor communications: "We're building a stronger system for tracking and proving outcomes." It demonstrates transparency, professionalism, and commitment to impact.

This process will reveal both what you already know and what you still need to find out. Do you have the data to back up your assumptions? If not, where could it come from? Some information may live in your client management system, while other data might exist externally, perhaps with a government agency, a local university, or a community partner.

Once you see the gaps, you can begin developing a data collection plan. Ask:

- What information do we need to measure true outcomes?
- How will we gather it: surveys, follow-ups, partner reports, or public data?
- Who will be responsible for collecting and reviewing it?
- How often will we revisit it to assess progress?

If you can find research that supports your intervention, such as a study, pilot project, or government evaluation, include it as evidence that your approach is proven or promising. This strengthens your credibility and gives donors confidence that your work aligns with best practices.

Next, build in feedback loops. Data shouldn't live in isolation or wait until the end of the year to be useful. Use what you learn to make small improvements in real time: adjust a curriculum, extend a service, or strengthen a partnership. When outcome measurement becomes part of daily operations, your organization learns faster, responds better, and celebrates progress more often.

Thinking about ROI

Once you're gathering outcomes, the next step is understanding their value. Return on investment (ROI) measures how much benefit results from the resources invested. The formula is simple:

ROI = (Gain – Cost) ÷ Cost

For example, if an organization invests $10,000 in a workforce program that leads to $50,000 in increased earnings and reduced public spending, the ROI is 400%. That means every $1 invested generates $4 in value.

While not every outcome can be converted into dollars, ROI thinking helps reframe your work in terms that resonate with funders, policymakers, and corporate partners. It communicates that your organization creates measurable community value.

Resources for Determining ROI

Understanding your ROI is learning what strategies generate the greatest impact for every dollar spent. Fortunately, there are reliable tools and frameworks that help nonprofits quantify both financial and social returns. Using these consistently transforms data into decision-making power.

Financial ROI Tools

For direct financial returns: fundraising efficiency, earned income ventures, or program cost recovery, these approaches can help you calculate and compare results:

- Cost–Benefit Analysis (CBA): Weighs total costs against measurable monetary benefits. Common for evaluating new programs, earned revenue ideas, or capital projects.
- RIMS II or IMPLAN Multipliers: Estimate the economic ripple effects of your organization's spending within the local economy, especially helpful when measuring community impact or job creation.
- Unit Cost Calculations: Divide total expenses by the number of clients served, classes offered, or outcomes achieved. This clarifies cost per service and supports pricing or funding decisions.
- Fundraising ROI Formula: *(Net revenue ÷ Fundraising expense = ROI ratio)*. A healthy nonprofit typically sees \$3–\$5 returned for every dollar spent on fundraising, though ratios vary by model.

Social and Programmatic ROI Tools

Social ROI (SROI) goes beyond dollars to include the measurable change created by your work:

- SROI Framework (Social Value UK/Stanford PACS): Converts social outcomes into financial proxies—for instance, the savings in healthcare or criminal justice systems resulting from prevention programs.[1]
- Logic Model Mapping: Links inputs, outputs, and outcomes to identify which activities yield the strongest results.
- Outcome Dashboards: Track quantitative and qualitative metrics (graduation rates, stable housing, improved mental health) to monitor progress over time.
- Longitudinal Data Comparison: Follows clients or communities over multiple years to measure sustained impact rather than one-time outputs.

Data Sources and Software

A few accessible resources can make ROI tracking more consistent and credible:

- IRS Form 990 data for peer benchmarking and overhead analysis.
- Guidestar/Candid for comparative financial and program performance.

- Program evaluation tools such as SurveyMonkey Impact, Tableau Public, Power BI, or Google Looker Studio for creating outcome dashboards.
- Donor management platforms like Bloomerang, Neon One, or Salesforce Nonprofit Cloud, which include ROI and retention reporting features.

Interpreting ROI

ROI numbers should be viewed in context. A higher ROI doesn't always mean greater mission impact. It may indicate underinvestment in staff or infrastructure. Likewise, a low ROI in early-stage programs may reflect intentional long-term investment. The goal is not to maximize profit but to understand how effectively your organization converts resources into results.

Remember: ROI is not a single metric; it's a mindset. By consistently tracking what you put in and what comes out, you create transparency, inform better decisions, and demonstrate the true value of your work to donors, boards, and communities alike.

Bringing It All Together

By completing a program inventory, mapping the input–output–outcome–ROI continuum, and identifying gaps, you've created the foundation for ongoing evaluation. The next step is to formalize it into a simple, repeatable evaluation plan.

Each year (or even quarterly), revisit your programs and ask:

- What results did we achieve?
- What changed for the people we serve?
- What data do we still need to capture?
- How can we use this information to improve outcomes and communicate impact more effectively?

Over time, this rhythm becomes second nature. Evaluation shifts from being a year-end scramble to a continuous process of learning, improving, and celebrating success. Remember, you don't have to start with perfect data, just honest effort and curiosity. Donors appreciate transparency and value organizations that are committed to learning. Your willingness to ask hard questions and build better systems for understanding impact tells them that their investment is in capable, forward-thinking hands. As you craft your board, you might consider reaching out to your local university to see if there are any scholars that might be interested in supporting your work and helping develop your outcome research.

Embedding Outcome Measurement into Organizational Culture

Outcome measurement thrives where curiosity lives. The best nonprofit leaders are constantly asking: *What worked? What didn't? Why? What does the data suggest we try next?* This mindset reframes measurement from compliance to discovery and from fear of failure to a commitment to learning and growth.

Yet one of the biggest challenges nonprofits face is that outcome tracking often becomes an afterthought. Too many organizations start worrying about data only at fiscal year-end, during a donor campaign, or when a funder suddenly requests results. The process becomes reactive, stressful, and incomplete.

To create lasting change, outcome measurement must be built into the very culture of the organization. When it's seen not as an external reporting requirement but as an internal learning tool, it stops being a burden and becomes a source of strength and alignment.

This cultural shift starts on the front lines. Staff and volunteers should view outcome tracking as a natural part of their daily work:

- In an after-school program, tutors might measure student reading levels at the start, midpoint, and end of each semester, not just to report progress but to adjust lesson plans in real time.
- In a healthcare organization, staff could document patient outcomes and follow-ups as part of standard intake and discharge, using that data to refine services and improve care.
- In a housing program, case managers might track milestones like job placement or rent stability during routine client check-ins; turning data collection into a moment to celebrate success rather than a once-a-year task.

Leaders and boards play a critical role in setting this tone. Boards that dedicate time in every meeting to review outcome progress signal that impact is as important as finances. Executive directors who celebrate small wins like the first student earning a scholarship or a community performance selling out show that measurement isn't about accountability alone; it's about pride, purpose, and progress.

This shift changes everything. It moves the focus from simply raising money to achieving meaningful results. Instead of tracking a fundraising thermometer that never quite fills up, the organization can celebrate the steady rise of real accomplishments: families housed, children succeeding, and communities thriving. That's what donors truly invest in: the joy of seeing their support create visible change. It helps everyone, from volunteers to board members, see how their work contributes to a shared mission. This sense of ownership builds morale, strengthens accountability, and demonstrates to donors that the organization is both intentional and effective in driving impact.

Creating a Feedback Loop between Operations, Development, and Marketing

Strong outcome measurement doesn't stop at collection; it depends on communication. Data must move freely between departments so that the entire organization speaks with one confident voice. In too many nonprofits, operations holds the data, development tells the story, and marketing amplifies it, but the flow between these teams is inconsistent or one-way. When that happens, valuable insights stay siloed, and opportunities to inspire donors or improve programs are missed. For example:

- From operations to development: frontline staff generate the raw evidence of impact on client progress, program milestones, and community change. When that information reaches the development team quickly and clearly, fundraisers can translate it into compelling donor messages that show tangible results and urgency.
- From development and marketing back to operations: fundraisers and communicators also gather important insights from donors, funders, and the public. When this feedback is shared with program teams, it helps shape how results are presented, what new outcomes are worth measuring, and how stories of impact can resonate more deeply with supporters.

This ongoing exchange creates a powerful feedback loop. For example, if the operations team tracks that 90% of clients secured stable housing, the development team can build a campaign around that success, while marketing can translate it into visuals, quotes, and stories that celebrate both the clients and the supporters who made it possible. In turn, donor reactions to that campaign (which stories resonate, which metrics inspire giving) can inform future data collection priorities for the program team.

When this loop is functioning well, every department contributes to a shared narrative of impact. Data becomes the engine of connection that links staff, donors, and communities in a common purpose.

Challenges to Measuring and Using Data

For most nonprofits, the hardest part of measuring impact is finding, cleaning, and comparing the data needed to prove results. Reliable information can be surprisingly difficult to obtain, especially when it comes to demonstrating long-term outcomes or calculating ROI. Public datasets may be outdated, incomplete, or scattered across multiple agencies. Even when information exists, it's rarely collected in consistent ways. Different organizations, counties, or states may use their own definitions, timelines, or reporting methods. Without common standards, it's difficult to compare "apples to apples" or to combine data across regions and programs.

The next challenge is data quality. Many nonprofits rely on manual tracking or disconnected systems, which can lead to gaps, duplicates, and inconsistencies. Staff turnover or limited training in data entry can make matters worse. Before any analysis can happen, data must be cleaned, verified, and aligned, work that requires both time and technical skill, often in short supply in the nonprofit sector.

Finally, some organizations face ethical and logistical barriers to collecting certain kinds of data, particularly when working with vulnerable populations or confidential information. Safety, privacy, and consent must come first, which can limit what's collected or shared.

These challenges don't mean outcomes or ROI can't be measured; they simply require thoughtful adaptation. Many organizations strengthen their analyses by using credible proxy data, pooling information from regional partners, or supplementing gaps with community or national research. When handled transparently, these methods can still tell a powerful and trustworthy story of impact.

Making Data Meaningful: Localizing and Humanizing Impact

When it comes to demonstrating impact, not all data is created equal. The most powerful numbers are those that feel relevant and personal to your audience. National statistics can provide context, but they rarely move donors to action. Billion-dollar figures sound impressive yet distant. What truly resonates are data points that connect directly to a donor's community, values, or lived experience.

For example, saying that domestic violence costs the U.S. economy billions each year feels abstract. But showing that it costs your county \$89 million in lost workplace productivity and \$210 million in taxpayer-funded services annually reframes the issue as immediate, local, and solvable. Suddenly, the problem isn't someone else's; it's theirs to help fix.

Major donors, policymakers, and corporate partners also want to understand the economic ripple effects of their support. Beyond direct ROI, they care about how their gift benefits the broader community, how it creates jobs, reduces public costs, or increases income and stability. A job training program, for instance, doesn't just change the lives of participants; it strengthens the local economy through increased spending, reduced public assistance, and higher tax revenues. Some nonprofits even use economic multipliers to show how every donated dollar circulates through the community, magnifying its effect.

To make your case even stronger, ROI conversations should capture both sides of the value equation: the costs avoided and the benefits created. Too often, organizations focus only on the harm prevented, like healthcare savings or reduced crime. Equally compelling is the positive growth that results: children succeeding in school, families achieving stability, or survivors re-entering the workforce. Together, these data points create a holistic and hopeful picture of impact.

When nonprofits move beyond broad national numbers and ground their evidence in meaningful, localized data, they build deeper trust and emotional connection. Donors see that their investment doesn't just make a difference somewhere; it makes a difference *here*. And that shift from abstract charity to concrete community transformation turns one-time gifts into long-term investments in change.

Case Study: Measuring Real Impact—The Economic Value of Ending Domestic Violence in Collier County

To understand how nonprofits can move beyond reporting activities to demonstrating true outcomes and ROI, consider the example of The Shelter for Abused Women & Children in Collier County, Florida.[2]

From Inputs to ROI

Like many nonprofits, The Shelter started by tracking the tangible resources invested in its mission: its inputs. These included more than $1.2 million in annual operating expenses, a dedicated staff of advocates and counselors, and thousands of volunteer hours. In 2023–4, they tracked and translated resources into outputs: 34,073 nights of safe shelter, 12,950 students in primary prevention classes, and over 18,769 hours of outreach support services for survivors and their families.[3]

While these numbers reflected tremendous effort, they did not yet tell the story of change. The Shelter's leadership wanted to understand whether their programs were producing measurable, lasting outcomes and to prove that the community's investment was paying off.

By analyzing outcomes, the organization found that 84% of survivors leaving the shelter achieved long-term safety and stability. Many secured permanent housing, gained employment, and avoided re-victimization. Families not only escaped immediate danger but also built foundations for independence.

When this analysis expanded to include ROI, the results were striking. Working with Sharity, The Shelter used local law enforcement statistics and medical and labor costs to create a formula for how to determine the costs of domestic violence on the community, outside of issues of personal health and safety.[4] The study estimated that Collier County taxpayers spent roughly $38.3 million annually on domestic-violence-related costs, from law enforcement and courts to healthcare and lost productivity. The Shelter's prevention and intervention programs saved the community an estimated $13 million each year. For every $1 invested, the programs generated between $1.80 and $7.00 in measurable community value, with an average taxpayer savings of $4.40 for every dollar spent.[5]

Translating the Data

This shift reframed the organization's impact along the continuum of change:

- Inputs: Funding, staff, volunteers, and facilities.
- Outputs: Shelter nights, counseling hours, and crisis calls.
- Outcomes: Survivors achieving long-term safety and self-sufficiency.
- ROI: Reduced public costs and increased community stability.

This case illustrates how outcome measurement transforms a nonprofit's story from activity to accountability. When The Shelter demonstrated its measurable economic and social returns, it gained stronger partnerships with local government, increased private funding, and heightened credibility with the business community.

By quantifying both human and financial impact, The Shelter proved that ending violence is not only the right thing to do, it's also a wise investment in community well-being. For every nonprofit, the lesson is clear: mastering the continuum from inputs to ROI isn't just about reporting data; it's about proving that your mission creates real, measurable change.

The Multiplier Effect: Nonprofits as Community Builders

Nonprofits are more than service providers; they are powerful economic drivers that strengthen communities. Every dollar they spend, job they create, or facility they build ripples through the local economy. This ripple, known as the multiplier effect, demonstrates how one organization's activities can boost jobs, increase household income, and expand the region's overall economic output.

When a nonprofit grows by adding buildings, hiring new employees, or expanding programs, its impact extends far beyond those directly served. Staff members earn wages that are spent locally on housing, food, and services. Vendors and contractors earn income that allows them to hire more workers. Families who benefit from nonprofit services gain stability, return to the workforce, and contribute to tax revenue. Taken together, these actions make nonprofits true community builders, creating stronger neighborhoods and healthier local economies.

Economists typically describe the multiplier effect in three parts: direct, indirect, and induced impact.

1 **Direct Impact**—This is the most visible level: the nonprofit's own spending on staff, supplies, and operations. When an organization pays salaries, purchases program materials, or contracts local services, those dollars immediately enter the local economy.

   - *Example:* A nonprofit hires teachers, administrators, and counselors, paying wages that support local households and generate income taxes.

2 **Indirect Impact**—These are the secondary ripples created when vendors and suppliers who receive nonprofit dollars reinvest them in their own operations.

   - *Example:* A nonprofit that hires a local construction company to build a new facility indirectly supports electricians, architects, landscapers, and suppliers of building materials.

3 **Induced Impact**—This third layer captures the community-wide effects as employees, vendors, and program graduates spend their earnings in the local economy.

   - *Example:* Staff, graduates, and families spend their income on groceries, housing, and transportation, fueling business growth and additional employment across the region (Figure 3.2).

An Example of the Multiplier Effect in Action

An economic impact report for a charter school building a new high school can demonstrate how nonprofits can measure and communicate this broader value. They can estimate that constructing a new high school and athletic facility would generate a $44 million increase in the region's GDP, create 285 construction jobs, and support 573 total jobs across all industries during the project. Once operational, the school's ongoing activities would add an estimated $7.8 million to the regional GDP each year and

Figure 3.2 The multiplier effects considers the larger ramifications of your organization's work on the broader community in numerous ways. This is not an exhaustive list. Be creative.

increase local household earnings by nearly $3 million annually. Whether it's a shelter expanding beds, a community center building a new gym, or a workforce program adding training capacity, each investment creates measurable returns for the broader economy.

Sharing the Bigger Picture

When nonprofits communicate results such as jobs created, household income increased, and GDP growth generated, they invite donors to see their work in a new light. A contribution isn't just helping people in need; it's fueling local economic growth.

By framing outcomes in both directions, both the costs avoided (reduced public spending, fewer emergency interventions) and the benefits created (jobs, earnings, and long-term stability), organizations present a full picture of their value. This dual framing not only resonates with donors and policymakers but also positions the nonprofit as a credible, high-value investment partner.

When funders see that their support strengthens both lives and local economies, they begin to view nonprofits not merely as charitable causes but as essential anchors of community and economic vitality (Figure 3.3).

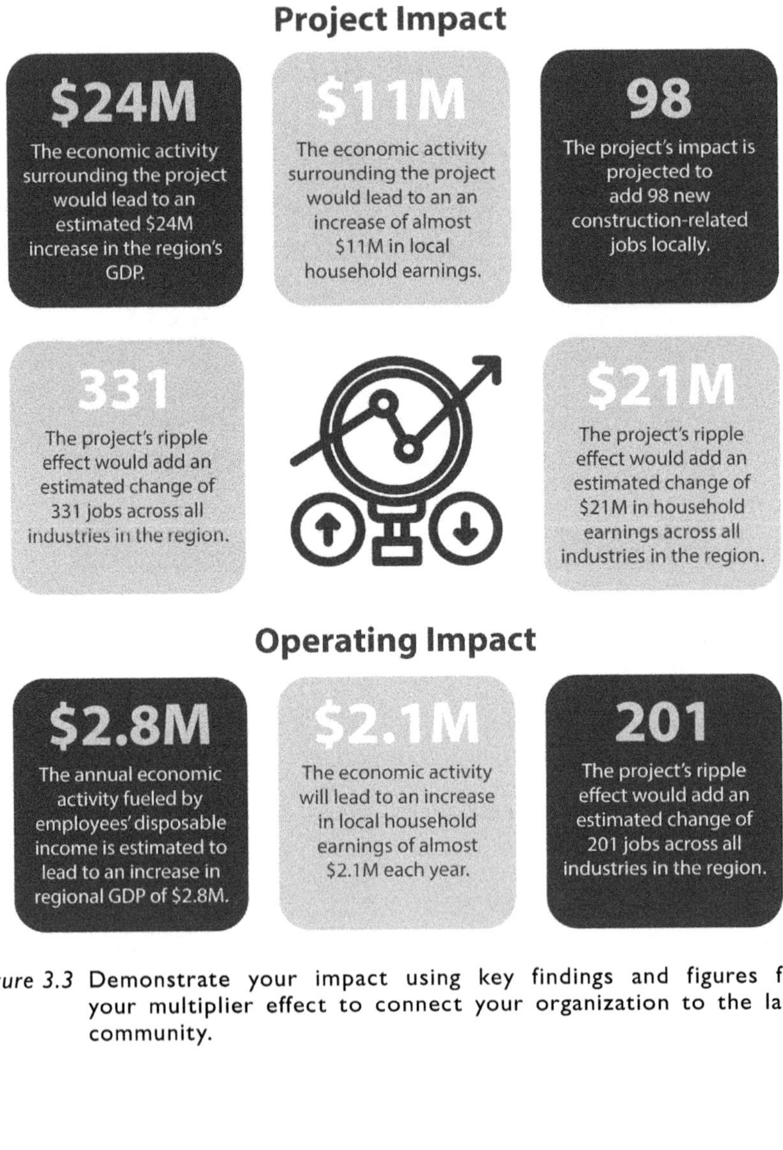

Figure 3.3 Demonstrate your impact using key findings and figures from your multiplier effect to connect your organization to the larger community.

Communicating Outcomes and Elevating Your Brand

Measuring outcomes is only half the story. The real power comes when those results are communicated clearly and creatively to the right audiences. Data hidden in a spreadsheet doesn't inspire action, but data brought to life through reports, research, pilots, and storytelling does.

Sharing your outcomes effectively transforms impact into influence. It builds donor confidence, attracts new partnerships, and strengthens your reputation as a results-driven organization. Whether through a polished outcome report, a university-backed research study, or a pilot project that demonstrates innovation, every communication is a chance to reinforce your credibility and elevate your brand.

Donors and funders want to see that your organization is leading change, shaping conversations, and setting new standards for excellence in your field. The following strategies show how to turn your results into compelling proof of impact, positioning your nonprofit as a trusted, high-performing community partner.

Let's begin with one of the most effective tools for sharing results: your outcome report.

Communicating with Outcome Reports

Like a company's annual report, a nonprofit's outcome report demonstrates performance, credibility, and value. Just as investors study a corporation's financials before investing, donors and funders look to outcome reports to see whether their gifts are achieving measurable impact.

A well-crafted outcome report shows how your organization has navigated challenges, stewarded resources, and delivered results. But publishing the report is only the beginning. It must also be shared, promoted, and celebrated. Announce it through newsletters, social media, presentations, and community events. Catalog it on your website, and make it easy for potential supporters to find. Each report is a public statement of accountability, success, and a marketing tool that elevates your organization's brand.

High-quality presentation matters. Outcome reports should reflect the professionalism of your mission: clear design, accessible language, strong visuals, and accurate data. Use fonts, graphics, and imagery that reflect your organization's personality and audience. An arts nonprofit might feature creative layouts and vibrant visuals; a healthcare or science-based organization might lean on clean data visuals and credible research citations. The goal is to create a signature look and feel that conveys expertise, integrity, and trustworthiness.

Condense key findings into visually engaging formats such as one-page infographics or dashboards that can be shared across multiple channels. For example:

> In 2024, 85% of our students improved their reading scores by at least one grade level.

Simple, powerful visuals make complex outcomes easy to digest and remember.

Research: Turning Data into Credibility

Strong research and data analysis not only demonstrate impact, but also help nonprofits make smarter, evidence-based decisions. You don't need a research department to start. Begin by tracking what you already do: who you serve, what outcomes they achieve, and what resources made that possible.

Small-scale evaluations such as participant surveys, pre- and post-program assessments, or follow-up interviews can uncover trends that improve programs and strengthen funding proposals. For instance, a literacy program might measure reading gains after six months, while a food security nonprofit could track families transitioning from emergency assistance to stable food access.

Partnerships with universities, research centers, or local businesses can further elevate your credibility. Academic or corporate collaborators bring technical expertise, data analysis, and the potential for co-branded studies that amplify visibility. Published findings or peer-reviewed research can help position your nonprofit as a thought leader, an organization that not only does good work but also advances knowledge in its field.

Responsible data collection is equally important. Protect participant privacy, obtain consent, and ensure evaluation methods never exploit or retraumatize those served. Ethical, transparent research builds trust and enhances your brand as a reliable community partner.

Pilots and Replication: Scaling What Works

Donors love to invest in proven ideas that can grow. Pilots and replication projects provide tangible proof that your work can scale effectively.

A pilot is a small-scale test of a new idea. It is an opportunity to assess feasibility, refine the model, and collect early data. For example, a workforce development nonprofit might pilot a new training track for one industry or neighborhood to measure job placement rates before expanding. These early results create powerful stories for funders who want to back innovation and learning.

Replication, on the other hand, demonstrates that success isn't limited to one location or population. When preparing to expand, document what made your original site effective, perhaps leadership, partnerships, funding mix, and staffing model, and what adaptations might be required elsewhere. Be honest about potential challenges. Transparency builds donor confidence and reinforces your reputation for integrity and accountability.

Both pilots and replication reports can be shared as short impact briefs, two to three pages summarizing results, lessons learned, and next steps. These are ideal tools for major donor meetings, grant proposals, or social media campaigns. They demonstrate not just that your programs work, but that they're ready to grow.

Thought Leadership: Using Data to Advance the Field

Collecting and analyzing outcomes is only part of the journey. What you do with that knowledge matters just as much. When nonprofits share their findings publicly, they don't just strengthen their reputation; they help advance the entire field, shape understanding, influence policy, and improve practice for everyone. Publishing your data, case studies, and lessons learned positions your organization as a *leader and innovator*, not just a service provider.

Thought leadership can take many forms: publishing op-eds or white papers, presenting at conferences, speaking on panels, or hosting community roundtables where you share your insights with peers. When you translate your data into accessible, compelling stories, showing what works, what doesn't, and why, you establish yourself as a trusted voice in your area of expertise.

This visibility does more than build credibility. It invites collaboration. Funders are drawn to organizations that push their field forward with fresh ideas, evidence, and transparency. Policymakers, researchers, and other nonprofits are more likely to partner with those who demonstrate humility and willingness to experiment, evaluate, and share.

If your organization has conducted research, piloted new models, or generated strong outcome data, consider taking those findings "on tour." Create a press release or visual summary that translates your results for the public. Offer to brief local reporters or civic leaders. Submit your insights to sector publications or professional journals. Speak about your process at conferences, not just your success, but also what you learned.

Your organization's data, paired with authentic storytelling, can help shape conversations far beyond your own programs. For instance, a housing nonprofit might publish findings showing how stable housing reduces healthcare costs; a youth organization could share longitudinal data demonstrating improved graduation rates and lifetime earnings.

The key is to rise above reporting and into *leadership*. When you contribute your findings to the larger dialogue, you show that your nonprofit is helping define what meaningful work looks like.

Narrative-Focused Outcome Sharing

Data tells what happened; stories tell *why it matters*. Balance the two. A two-minute video of a client sharing how their life changed can move donors more deeply than a spreadsheet. Use multimedia like videos, photos, and testimonials to bring outcomes to life.

Different audiences may connect to different aspects of your impact. A corporate partner might respond to ROI and job creation; an individual donor might connect more with a story of personal transformation. Tailor your message to what your audience values most. When outcome reports reveal surprising findings or address issues of public interest, they can capture media attention and elevate your brand far beyond the nonprofit sector.

Bringing It All Together

Each of these strategies—outcome reports, research, pilots, replication, and storytelling—serves as a proof point reinforcing why your organization exists and how it creates measurable change. Together, they transform your communications from fundraising appeals into evidence-based stories of impact.

When done well, these tools elevate your nonprofit's reputation from being one of many service providers to being a leading organization that drives results, shares knowledge, and inspires investment.

The most compelling fundraising narratives are rooted in truth, backed by data, and told with vision. Use every report, pilot, and partnership as an opportunity to demonstrate not just that your work matters, but that it works. Here is a handy guide to some common pitfalls to avoid:

Things to Avoid in Measuring and Sharing Outcomes

- **Confusing outputs with outcomes**
  Counting activities (meals served, classes taught, books donated) without showing the *impact* (families moving out of food insecurity, students improving reading levels, clients finding stable housing) leaves donors questioning the real difference made.

- **Sharing metrics that don't matter**
  It's tempting to track what's easiest to measure, but vanity metrics (like event attendance or social media responses) don't always connect to mission success or donor priorities.
- **Overcomplicating the data**
  Donors want clarity, not a dense research report. Presenting too many statistics, technical jargon, or confusing charts can obscure the story rather than illuminate it. Consider testing your promotional materials with board members to see what is most impactful.
- **Ignoring qualitative evidence**
  Finding a balance between heart and mind is key. Numbers matter, but stories and lived experiences give outcomes depth and heart. Relying solely on data can make reports feel detached. Mix stories with outcome reports to demonstrate the impact that the organization has had numerous times over.
- **Failing to recognize specific outcomes with donor impact**
  Donors want to see how *their specific contribution* made a difference. For large-scale donors, consider writing a specific impact report just for them to demonstrate how their willingness to open a library in a transitional housing unit or clinic for an animal shelter has had a specific impact.
- **Not reporting failures or challenges**
  Only sharing successes can feel inauthentic. Donors value transparency about what didn't work and how the organization is adapting. Honest reflection builds credibility. If a program was not a success, share what went wrong, and most importantly, how you plan to use the knowledge gained to retool for future success. For example, if a morning reading program was a failure, do research to determine why and report back. Perhaps you determined 7:30am was unappealing, even with free breakfast, for the program, and after interviewing program clients, you are switching to an afternoon or evening program. It demonstrates a dedication to the mission statement and a connection with the clients, rather than plowing forward with failing plans.
- **Treating outcome reports as one-off or year-end tasks**
  Waiting until grant deadlines or annual reports to measure impact means missed opportunities. Outcome tracking should be continuous. It can help give immediate feedback on programs so changes can be made if necessary. If unique outcomes emerge, perhaps consider novel ways of communicating this to the general public, donors, or other specific audience targets to build goodwill

Summary—Proof Builds Trust

Measuring outcomes is the foundation of a nonprofit's credibility and long-term success. Donors, funders, and partners increasingly expect proof that their support creates measurable change, and organizations that can clearly articulate outcomes stand out in a crowded field.

Outcome measurement strengthens programs, informs strategic decisions, and creates a culture of accountability and pride within the organization. Throughout this chapter, we explored practical ways to demonstrate outcomes, from ROI calculations and economic impact studies to outcome reports, pilots, and thought leadership. We also discussed how to avoid common pitfalls, such as confusing outputs with outcomes, overloading reports with data, or treating measurement as an afterthought.

The central theme is clear: when measurement is embedded into daily operations, it transforms from a burden into a source of strength. It motivates staff, reassures donors, and reinforces progress toward the mission. When outcomes are woven into every part of the organization: planning, programs, fundraising, and communications, they create a narrative of impact that is both authentic and compelling. This combination of proof and story builds trust, inspires investment, and strengthens relationships with donors and partners who want to see tangible results.

Measuring outcomes is about accountability and understanding transformation. It's how nonprofits align every decision, resource, and relationship around purpose and proof. When data flows freely across teams, connecting operations, development, and marketing, it turns information into insight and insight into action.

As you reflect on this chapter, consider:

- How often do we discuss outcomes in staff meetings compared to finances?
- What small data habit could we start this month to make tracking easier?
- Which outcomes do we celebrate, and which do we overlook?

The work of tracking, analyzing, and communicating outcomes lays the groundwork for the next stage of nonprofit success: building deeper relationships, scaling programs, and leveraging resources strategically. In the next chapter, we'll explore how to translate these insights into actionable strategies for engaging donors, forging long-term partnerships, and ensuring every dollar invested produces both measurable impact and lasting change.

Key Takeaways

- **Measure what matters.** Focus on life changes, not activity counts.
- **Use data to tell stories.** Numbers and narratives together drive deeper understanding.

- **Link outcomes to strategy.** Every goal in your plan should have a measurable result.
- **Be transparent.** Share successes *and* lessons learned, as authenticity earns trust.
- **Outcomes attract investment.** Funders back organizations that can demonstrate results.

Progress Check

After reading this chapter, rate where your organization is on a scale of one to five, with one being that your organization does not have this component, or is just beginning to work on it, and five being that your organization is fully operational and has this element ready for vetting by a major donor. Out of a maximum of five points, the goal is to score at least 20.

Notes:

Citations

1 Social Value UK. (2020). A guide to social return on investment (SROI). Social Value UK. https://socialvalueuk.org/wp-content/uploads/2020/08/SROI-Final-Report-Assured-12Aug20.pdf.

Stanford Center on Philanthropy and Civil Society (PACS). (n.d.). Stanford Social Innovation Review (SSIR). Stanford University. https://pacscenter.stanford.edu/resources/ssir/.

2 Wick, Carol, MS; Parada, Ariadna. (2020) Estimating the Local Impact of Intimate Partner Violence and the Value of Domestic Violence Programming: A Study of Collier County, Florida in 2018.

3 The Naples Center. "The Shelter Impact Report, 2023–4." 2024. https://www.flipsnack.com/theshelternaples/2024-the-shelter-impact-report/full-view.html.

4 The Shelter. 2024. "The 2023 Estimated Cost of Domestic Violence in Collier County." https://naplesshelter.org/wp-content/uploads/2024/05/2023-Estimated-Cost-of-Domestic-Violence-in-Collier-County.pdf.

5 The Shelter. 2024. "The cost of domestic violence in Collier County." https://naplesshelter.org/COST/.

Chapter 4

Building a Quality Team

The Team Factor: Building the People Who Make the Mission Possible

No nonprofit succeeds on passion alone. Even the best plan will fail without the right people to bring it to life. A strong team, including executive leaders, board members, staff, volunteers, and fundraisers, forms the backbone of a healthy, investable organization. Donors know this. When donors look at your organization, they are considering your mission and team they're investing in. They want to know that leadership is stable, governance is strong, staff are competent, and culture is healthy. These are the trust indicators that turn one-time gifts into long-term investments. Building the right team is an HR function and a fundraising strategy.

Whether you're launching a new nonprofit or rebuilding one in transition, your team is the most critical investment you'll make. The goal is to design a structure and culture that works in practice, not just on paper.

Leadership and Board: Setting the Tone for Trust

Every organization reflects its leadership. The executive director and senior team establish the pace, tone, and standards that ripple throughout the organization. Donors and funders look for stability and credibility here. Leaders who can articulate vision, manage resources wisely, and adapt under pressure.

Equally vital is the board. Strong boards open doors, bring expertise, and amplify credibility. A donor's first question after reviewing your mission is often, *Who's on your board?* They're not just asking out of curiosity; they're looking for signals of influence, oversight, and community reach.

Boards should be composed not only of mission believers but also of strategic partners who understand their role: governance, fundraising, and ambassadorship. When recruiting, seek people who can champion your cause in rooms you can't yet enter.

DOI: 10.4324/9781003746218-5

Staff: Turning Plans into Impact

An operational plan is only as strong as the people who carry it out. Staff bring the mission to life through daily work that often stretches far beyond their job descriptions. Hiring well means looking for both skill and alignment with people who understand *why* your organization exists, not just *what* it does.

Create clear job descriptions and invest in onboarding. Too many nonprofits hire quickly and hope for the best. Instead, give new employees context: why their role matters, how success is measured, and how their work contributes to outcomes. A thoughtful onboarding process can reduce turnover and accelerate performance more effectively than any raise.

Growth-oriented nonprofits also plan ahead for team development. If your budget allows, build capacity in areas that sustain growth: data management, donor relations, operations, and communications. If it doesn't, develop partnerships and interim contracts to fill those gaps until permanent staff are feasible.

Fundraising and Development: The Other Half of the Team

The fundraising team, whether a single development director or a full advancement department, is as vital as the program staff. They keep the engine running. Too often, organizations underinvest in development and then wonder why they struggle to grow.

Fundraising is ultimately about building relationships. That requires skilled communicators who can connect donor interests to measurable impact and a board willing to support them. If your development function isn't strong, your fundraising results won't be either.

When resources are limited, consider fractional fundraisers or shared services. It's better to have experienced support part-time than inexperienced help full-time. Build your development function intentionally, aligning roles with your financial goals and capacity to steward relationships.

Volunteers: Extending Your Reach

Volunteers can be one of your organization's greatest assets if managed with intention and respect. They are not free labor; they are partners in the mission. A well-designed volunteer program multiplies your reach, builds community investment, and often creates your next generation of donors and board members.

Strong volunteer engagement begins with structure. Define roles clearly, outlining expectations, skills required, and time commitments. Provide orientation and training just as you would for paid staff. Volunteers represent your brand in the community, and their experience shapes how others perceive your organization. When expectations are vague or oversight is minimal, well-meaning volunteers can burn out or, worse, damage relationships or credibility.

Risk management is also essential. Conduct background checks when appropriate, especially for volunteers working with children, vulnerable adults, or animals. Review insurance coverage to ensure volunteers are protected under your liability policy. Safety and compliance should be built into your volunteer handbook, not added as an afterthought.

Equity and inclusion must also guide volunteer recruitment and engagement. Too often, volunteerism reflects privilege. Those with flexible time and financial security are the ones who can "give back." Expanding access means thinking creatively: offering shorter shifts, virtual roles, or skill-based micro-projects that allow people from different backgrounds and schedules to participate. Partner with community groups, faith institutions, and schools to reach volunteers who reflect the people you serve.

Representation matters. When your volunteer team mirrors the diversity of your community, it sends a powerful message of belonging. It deepens trust and helps avoid the "outsider helper" dynamic that can unintentionally reinforce inequity. Inclusion isn't just about who joins; it's about how they are treated once they do. That means ensuring every volunteer feels valued, respected, and part of the mission, not just an extra set of hands.

Recognition and feedback are vital. Express gratitude often, through handwritten notes, shout-outs in newsletters, or small appreciation events. But also listen. Invite volunteers to share their experiences, insights, and ideas for improvement. Volunteers often see needs and opportunities staff might miss. A culture of mutual respect turns volunteers into lifelong advocates and donors. When managed well, volunteers strengthen the organization's capacity, extend its visibility, and deepen its credibility.

Culture: The Glue That Holds It All Together

Your culture is not just who you are internally. It's what donors, clients, and partners experience every time they interact with your organization. It shapes how your team works, how you hire, how you communicate, and how you live your mission. A strong culture is your most powerful brand.

When a nonprofit clearly defines its culture and values, it attracts the right people, such as staff, board members, and volunteers who align with its mission and energy. Your public identity through your messaging, website, and social presence should reflect this. If your work is grassroots and fast-moving, your culture should feel bold and action-oriented. If you focus on policy or research, your culture might highlight collaboration, reflection, and evidence-driven rigor. Brand clarity helps potential hires and donors know what kind of organization you are.

Culture and brand also serve as recruitment and retention tools. Nonprofits can't always compete with corporate salaries, but they can offer something more meaningful: purpose, growth, and belonging. A clear, authentic brand signals that your organization is a place where people can make a difference *and* develop professionally. That sense of shared mission builds loyalty, reduces turnover, and strengthens team performance.

Equity in Action

Your culture must reflect your mission. If your organization advocates for fairness, inclusion, or compassion in the world, those same principles must live inside your walls. Nothing erodes trust faster, internally or externally, than a nonprofit that preaches justice but practices inequity.

Equity begins with how you treat your people. Pay and benefits should be fair, transparent, and aligned with the market. Staff should have access to growth opportunities, regular raises, and advancement based on merit and contribution, not simply tenure or proximity to leadership. Attention to potential race or gender disparities in hiring, promotion, and pay offers true integrity. A nonprofit that mirrors the values it fights for earns the respect of staff, funders, and the community alike.

Diversity, equity, and inclusion are not checkboxes or statements on a website. They are not a political statement, nor are they optional in the nonprofit world. Call them by whatever terms you want; they are ongoing practices that make your organization stronger, more credible, and more connected to the communities you serve. Diversity brings different perspectives and lived experiences into the room. Equity ensures fair access to opportunity and voice. Inclusion creates safety and the ability for every person to participate fully, be heard, and influence decisions.

Real commitment requires continuous reflection and accountability. This might include anonymous surveys, facilitated discussions, or external consultants who can help identify blind spots. Boards and executives should lead this process, not delegate it. A credible organization demonstrates its values in governance, leadership composition, and daily interactions, not just in programs or outreach.

Building a Culture of Belonging

A healthy culture is built on connection. Celebrate milestones. Recognize contributions publicly. Offer flexibility when possible. Create systems that allow people to express ideas or concerns safely and without fear of retaliation. Psychological safety, the belief that it's safe to speak up, is one of the strongest predictors of high-performing teams.

Organizational culture is not merely a "soft" issue; it is a critical indicator for fundraising. Donors and funders observe stability and are deterred by high turnover. A vibrant culture signals that your organization is well-managed, disciplined, and sustainable. It demonstrates that you prioritize your employees, which, in turn, assures donors that their investments will be handled with similar care.

Ultimately, culture is the glue that holds everything together: your brand, your mission, your people, and your credibility. When lived intentionally, it becomes one of your greatest strategic advantages and one of the clearest indicators to donors that your organization is built to last.

Evolving the Team as You Grow

Growth changes everything. Most nonprofits begin with a handful of people doing everything: writing grants, answering phones, delivering services, and cleaning up after events, often for little or no pay. They are driven by mission, not money, and their effort and sacrifice form the heart of the organization. But as the organization matures, passion alone is no longer enough. The work becomes more complex, the stakes get higher, and the skill sets required to sustain growth change.

This evolution can be deeply personal and often painful. The office manager who once ran every program may not have the experience to oversee a multi-site budget. The bookkeeper who handled receipts in a shoebox may struggle with audit requirements. And sometimes, the hardest transition of all involves the founder.

Founder Syndrome

"Founder syndrome" occurs when the identity of an organization becomes inseparable from the person who created it. Founders are often visionaries. They've built something from nothing, navigated early crises, and carried the mission on their backs. But the same qualities that drive a startup phase—intensity, control, and personal ownership—can become barriers to scale. Successful transition requires letting go, which is one of the hardest things for any leader to do.

A founder's departure, or even the redistribution of authority, must be handled with extraordinary care. Donors, staff, and clients watch closely for signs of instability. The goal is not to erase the founder's legacy but to honor it while ensuring the organization can thrive beyond one person. This means succession planning early, transparent communication, and building a leadership culture that values systems over personalities. When handled well, founder transitions are a signal to funders that the organization is built to last.

These transitions are never simple and rarely without emotion. The following example illustrates how one organization navigated this shift with integrity and what happens when it's done well.

Case Study: When Passion Outgrows Capacity—Navigating Founder Transitions

When a youth prevention program launched, it was little more than a borrowed office, a donated laptop, and one woman's determination to help survivors of domestic violence find housing and hope. For the first five years, the founder did everything: grant writing, case management, payroll, and even painting walls between client appointments. Her leadership was the heartbeat of the organization, and donors adored her.

But success brought growth. Within a decade, the organization had a staff of 30, a multimillion-dollar budget, and new federal reporting requirements. The board began asking for performance dashboards and risk assessments. What had once been a hands-on, flexible organization now needed systems, policies, and professional management.

The founder struggled. Meetings felt bureaucratic. She missed the personal contact with clients and resented the new executive director the board hired to "help formalize operations." Staff felt torn between loyalty to the founder and accountability to new leadership. Tension began to show in staff turnover and donor unease.

A turning point came when a longtime board member facilitated a structured transition process. They celebrated the founder's achievements publicly and established a new role for her, Founder Emeritus, focused on storytelling and donor engagement, areas that played to her strengths and legacy. The board invested in coaching for both the founder and the new CEO, helping each define boundaries and communication norms.

The process was not easy. There were emotional moments and tough conversations, but the outcome was transformative. The organization retained its heart while gaining the infrastructure needed to grow responsibly. Donors praised the transparency, and the organization's credibility deepened.

Sustainable nonprofits evolve beyond the vision of one person. Honoring a founder's legacy while empowering new leadership is one of the hardest, but most important, transitions an organization can make. Donors notice when it's handled with integrity and foresight; they also notice when it's not. In the end, a successful transition is about preserving purpose. The organization that learns to evolve its leadership without losing its soul is the one that endures.

Managing and Supporting Staff with Lived Experience

Many nonprofits, especially those in social services, advocacy, or community-based work, employ staff who bring *lived experience* directly connected to the mission. They are survivors of violence, individuals in recovery, or those who have faced homelessness, foster care, or discrimination. These employees offer a level of empathy, credibility, and insight that can't be replicated through training alone. Their voices strengthen program design, deepen community trust, and help clients feel truly seen and understood.

This powerful strength also requires careful leadership. When the personal and professional overlap too closely, lines can blur, and both staff and clients can be affected. The leader's role is to honor lived experience while maintaining the professionalism, structure, and accountability every mission-driven organization needs to thrive.

The key is balance. Employment must remain professional, not therapeutic. Staff who carry personal histories related to their work may face triggers or emotional strain. Supervisors should ensure that support systems are in place, including regular supervision, access to counseling, and debriefing after difficult cases. These should be standard practice, not optional benefits. These practices normalize self-care and prevent burnout or retraumatization.

It's equally important to establish clear professional expectations. Staff with lived experience are employees, not clients. Their roles, responsibilities, and performance standards should be defined in writing and applied consistently. When leaders avoid accountability conversations out of fear of appearing unsupportive, they risk undermining the stability that both employees and clients rely on.

Leaders can model healthy boundaries by reinforcing that *caring for clients doesn't mean carrying their pain.* Empathy drives good service, but over-identification can erode objectivity, create dependency, or lead to boundary violations. Creating a culture where seeking help is viewed as strength, not weakness, empowers staff to work sustainably and model resilience for others.

The message should be compassionate and firm: *we value your experience, and we also expect professionalism and self-awareness.* Supporting staff means equipping them, not rescuing them. With structure, supervision, and clear expectations, employees with lived experience can transform personal healing into professional impact.

The Emotional Work of Management

Managing a growing team in a mission-driven organization is emotionally demanding. Nonprofit leaders often carry not only operational responsibility but also the weight of other people's purpose and pain. The transition from "we'll do anything to get it done" to a more structured, sustainable workplace can feel like a loss. Longtime staff may resent new hires with specialized skills or formal titles. Others may feel left behind as systems replace improvisation.

Leaders must manage these dynamics with empathy and firmness, acknowledging past sacrifices while keeping the focus on what the mission needs now. Difficult conversations about role shifts or reassignments are part of professionalizing an organization. Avoiding them only prolongs frustration and hinders growth.

A good leader approaches these moments with honesty and gratitude: "You helped us get here. Now our next chapter requires new expertise, and I want to find a way to honor your contributions as we grow." When people feel seen and respected, even in transition, they're far more likely to remain allies of the mission.

Onboarding: Preparing for Success

Nonprofits are notorious for throwing new hires into the deep end and hoping they swim. For my first Executive Director job, my "training" was a two-hour orientation from the Chief Financial Officer (CFO) who ended by saying, *Good luck*. I remember the panic of realizing how much responsibility I carried and how little guidance I had. That experience shaped how I approach onboarding to this day.

Every new team member deserves to start with clarity, context, and connection. A strong onboarding process helps people understand not just *what* to do, but *why* it matters. It should include:

- A clear overview of the organization's mission, values, and culture
- Hands-on training in systems, compliance, and daily workflows
- A mentor or peer partner who can answer practical and cultural questions
- Defined success metrics and regular check-ins for the first 90 days

Effective onboarding starts before day one. Send a welcome email, outline expectations, and provide reading or resources. During the first week, focus on integration, not just information. Introduce new hires to colleagues, share organizational stories, and help them see their place in the larger mission.

Onboarding should also be seen as an ongoing process, not a one-day event. Over the first six months, provide access to training, webinars, and professional development opportunities. Encourage employees to take a few hours each month to build new skills or pursue certifications relevant to their role. When staff feel invested in and supported, they're more likely to stay, grow, and contribute creatively.

Managing Burnout and Building Sustainability

Mission-driven people are often the first to overextend themselves. The work feels too important to pause, and "no" feels like betrayal. But exhaustion is not a strategy; it's a warning sign. Leaders must watch for burnout: fatigue, irritability, withdrawal, and declining quality of work.

Preventing burnout requires intentional management. Set boundaries, model balance, and normalize rest. Encourage staff to take time off, use mental health resources, and disconnect outside work hours. Consider flexibility in scheduling, such as remote work or occasional mental health days. When people feel trusted and supported, productivity and retention improve dramatically.

Sustainability also depends on systems. Clear policies, shared tools, and defined workflows save time and reduce stress. Build these habits before you're overwhelmed, and make feedback routine. Regular check-ins allow staff to voice challenges before they turn into crises.

A sustainable organization isn't one that runs on sacrifice. It's one that runs on structure, trust, and care. Evolving a team is never easy. It requires courage to make hard decisions, humility to accept change, and compassion to honor those who carried the organization through its early days. Managing people is not a distraction from the mission; it *is* the mission. Because when your team is healthy, focused, and equipped, your impact multiplies.

Finding the Balance Between the Right Staff and Enough Staff

On paper, building a great team seems simple: hire the most qualified people who care deeply about the mission. In reality, it's far more complicated. Nonprofits must constantly balance two questions: *Do we have the right people?* and *Do we have enough of them?* Hire too many too soon, and financial strain can lead to painful cuts that damage morale and erode trust. Hire too few, and staff burn out while programs and opportunities suffer.

A smart staffing strategy aligns growth with both mission goals and financial capacity. Every new hire adds not only a salary but also costs for onboarding, supervision, benefits, equipment, and workspace. Sustainable staffing means growing thoughtfully, adding people when the organization can support them well, not just when the need feels urgent.

Benchmarking can help. Study peer organizations of similar size and scope. How many staff do they have? What does their structure look like across fundraising, programs, and operations? How are responsibilities divided between leadership, finance, HR, data, and communications? Understanding these patterns can highlight where your own organization is overextended or under-resourced.

For example, you may discover that comparable organizations employ a dedicated development manager or data specialist, roles that improve performance but may not exist in your current structure. Generally, nonprofits with under $100,000 in revenue operate with four to five employees; those with $500,000 to $1 million average about a dozen; and larger organizations often add 25–40 people for every $10 million in revenue. While every nonprofit is unique, these ratios offer a reference point for reasonable expectations.

The best approach is phased hiring, adding positions gradually and intentionally. Start with roles that directly advance strategic priorities, then set review checkpoints (at six or twelve months) to assess performance, capacity, and financial impact. If growth outpaces resources, pause before expanding further. If revenue and output remain strong, plan the next hire.

Don't overlook indirect costs. More staff means more equipment, software licenses, training, and management time. Expanding too quickly without accounting for those costs can quietly destabilize even the healthiest budgets.

Ultimately, staffing is about scaling sustainably. The goal is to build a skilled team to fulfill the mission effectively without overreaching the organization's capacity. Regularly assessing staff workload, fundraising performance, and budget forecasts ensures that your human capital grows in step with your financial and strategic reality.

Fundraising Takes a Team: The Interdependence of the CEO, CFO, COO, and Development Officer

Fundraising success is the product of a well-synchronized executive team. In strong nonprofits, the CEO, CFO, COO, and Chief Philanthropy Officer (or Development Director) each play a vital role, and the organization thrives only when these roles are aligned. When they operate in silos, even the best fundraising plan can fail.

The CEO: Setting the Vision and Engaging the Board

The CEO's role is to define the organization's long-term strategy and ensure that fundraising aligns with it. They are responsible for creating and maintaining the business plan that drives all operational and fundraising decisions.

A CEO who understands their role in fundraising recognizes that donors give to a compelling vision, not just to programs. That vision must be shared, credible, and backed by a plan that the CEO helps craft and communicate.

Equally important is board engagement. When the CEO develops the strategic plan collaboratively, board members feel ownership. They become more willing to open doors, make introductions, and champion the mission publicly. A disengaged board, by contrast, leaves the development staff isolated and unsupported.

The CFO: Turning Vision into Numbers

The CFO translates the strategic plan into a financial roadmap. They forecast expenses, model revenue growth, and build multi-year budgets that anticipate both opportunities and risks. A strong CFO with nonprofit experience understands the complexities of restricted and unrestricted funding, cost reimbursement, and cash-flow timing. They can explain to funders why reserves matter, demonstrate financial transparency, and ensure the organization is sustainable.

When the CFO partners closely with the Chief Philanthropy Officer (CPO), they provide the data needed for credible asks: multi-year projections, funding gaps, and clear outcomes tied to investment. This partnership helps donors see that their contribution is an investment, not a donation.

The COO: Measuring What Matters

The COO is often overlooked in fundraising conversations, yet their contribution is essential. The COO ensures that programs deliver measurable outcomes, not just outputs. Donors don't want to know only how many meals were served or how many clients attended workshops; they want proof of transformation.

By leading outcome measurement and data collection, the COO provides the evidence the development team needs to make the case for investment. They also maintain compliance, oversee program quality, and capture the human stories that make fundraising emotionally resonant. A strong COO not only ensures program integrity but also validates that the organization's work truly achieves its mission of turning donor dollars into documented impact.

The Chief Philanthropy Officer: Turning Plans and Data into Support

Once the CEO sets the direction, the CFO quantifies the need, and the COO documents results, the Chief Philanthropy Officer (CPO) turns that alignment into action. Their job is to design and execute the fundraising strategy: cultivating relationships, managing donor pipelines, and ensuring stewardship.

The CPO can only succeed if the other executives deliver what's required: a realistic plan, a credible budget, and measurable impact. Without those inputs, the fundraiser is "handed a number and told to go find the money," an approach that leads to burnout and turnover. When fully supported, the CPO becomes the organization's storyteller and connector, linking mission, outcomes, and opportunity to the right donors at the right time.

How the Team Works Together

Each of these leaders holds a crucial piece of the puzzle:

- **The CEO** ensures the mission is clear and compelling.
- **The CFO** builds the financial model to sustain it.
- **The COO** proves the work is effective.
- **The CPO** invites others to invest in that success.

When they plan, budget, measure, and communicate together, fundraising shifts from an annual scramble to a long-term strategy. Donors sense cohesion and confidence, and they respond in kind.

Building the Right Fundraising Team

If there's one area where nonprofits consistently get it wrong, it's fundraising staffing. Many organizations still hire based on personality rather than performance potential, looking for someone "great with people" and expecting them to handle everything from grant writing to galas.

Then they wonder why they fail.

Let's be blunt: in a for-profit company, no one would hire one person to manage sales, communications, project management, and government relations, and expect record revenue. Yet many nonprofits routinely hire one "development director" for the salary of a middle manager and load them with every fundraising responsibility imaginable.

The Problem with the "One-Person Fundraising Department"

This grassroots mentality—"we'll make it work with one good person"—is one of the biggest reasons organizations plateau. Fundraising is an ecosystem. Grant writing, donor cultivation, events, digital engagement, and corporate partnerships all require distinct expertise. When one person is expected to master them all, burnout is inevitable, and progress stalls around the 18-month mark.

The result? The "development revolving door." A talented but overextended staff member wins a few quick donations, then hits a wall and leaves, only to repeat the cycle at another organization.

Fundraising should be viewed exactly like revenue generation in the business world: disciplined, strategic, and never the first thing cut from the budget. Donor development requires both relationship building and systems management. Without infrastructure and staffing specialization, even the most passionate professionals can't succeed.

The solution isn't to hire fast; it's to hire smart, build a sustainable structure, and grow it over time. Start by understanding the three core roles that form the foundation of a healthy fundraising department.

Major Gifts Officer (MGO)—The Relationship Architect

A strong MGO manages the organization's most important donors: individuals, foundations, and corporations capable of giving transformational gifts. Their job is to strategically manage a portfolio of 75–150 prospects, cultivating long-term relationships that align donor passion with organizational need.

An effective MGO combines empathy and storytelling with project management and data discipline. They:

- Develop individualized cultivation and solicitation plans for each prospect.
- Collaborate with executives, program staff, and the board to align proposals with impact.
- Track donor interactions, forecast revenue, and maintain accurate CRM records.
- Ensure each donor receives personalized stewardship and evidence of impact.

In short, an MGO functions like a strategic sales director for philanthropy focused on relationships that generate the highest return on investment.

Development Operations—The Engine behind the System

Every strong fundraising department relies on operations professionals who keep the systems running smoothly. A Development Operations Manager (sometimes called an Advancement Associate) handles the critical behind-the-scenes work that enables fundraisers to focus on donor relationships instead of data entry.

Their role centers on precision, analysis, and efficiency. They:

- Manage the donor database (CRM), ensuring clean, accurate, and complete records.
- Process gifts and acknowledgments promptly, maintaining donor trust.
- Generate regular fundraising reports, analyzing trends and return on investment (ROI) by campaign or channel.
- Collaborate with marketing and finance teams to align communications and accounting.
- Support events, mailings, and stewardship activities by providing data and logistics.

This position is the infrastructure of fundraising, the operational counterpart to the MGO's relational work. A good operations person makes the entire department more effective, ensuring nothing falls through the cracks and every donor touchpoint is timely and professional.

Annual Fund Manager—The Pipeline Builder

The Annual Fund is the backbone of sustainable philanthropy. It builds the donor base that fuels every other campaign. A dedicated Annual Fund Manager designs and implements the year-round plan for broad-based giving, including managing appeals, volunteer committees, digital outreach, and stewardship.

This role focuses on growth and engagement, not just transactions. A strong Annual Fund Manager:

- Develops a multichannel solicitation calendar (email, mail, social media, and events).
- Sets participation and revenue goals, then tracks progress throughout the year.
- Manages donor segmentation and personalized appeals to retain and upgrade givers.
- Coordinates volunteers and ambassadors who help extend the organization's reach.
- Works with communications to ensure consistent messaging across all platforms.

The Annual Fund Manager builds the pipeline of future major donors, cultivating consistent givers who deepen their involvement over time. When paired with an MGO and strong operations staff, this role transforms scattered fundraising into a cohesive strategy.

Right-Sizing and Measuring the Team

The right mix and number of fundraising staff depend on organizational size, donor base, and funding diversity. Smaller organizations may combine these functions under one or two people, but as revenue grows, specialization becomes essential.

Track fundraising ROI to determine when to expand. As a general rule, every dollar spent on development should yield \$3–\$5 in revenue. Monitor donor retention rates, campaign performance, and staff workload. If core priorities like stewardship or reporting start slipping, it's time to invest in capacity.

The Formula for Sustainable Fundraising Growth

1 **Hire slow, train well, and support fully.**
2 **Build infrastructure first.** Technology, data hygiene, and systems matter as much as relationships.
3 **Add staff based on strategy, not panic.** Hire to strengthen specific functions as funding allows.
4 **Treat fundraising as an investment, not an expense.** It pays for everything else.

Fundraising staff are not overhead; they are the growth engine. The organizations that understand this scale and flourish.

Building Fundraising Infrastructure for Sustainable Growth

As organizations grow, so must their fundraising infrastructure. Larger nonprofits naturally require more specialized roles, with each focused on a distinct area of relationship building, communication, or data management. Growth brings complexity: more donors to steward, more partnerships to maintain, and more opportunities to manage strategically.

The evolution of a fundraising department should be intentional, not reactive. Early-stage nonprofits often rely on generalists who wear many hats. As budgets expand, structure and specialization become essential. A maturing organization will eventually need staff dedicated to core functions such as corporate partnerships, strategic alliances, annual giving, and institutional support.

For example, a Director of Corporate and Foundation Relations can focus exclusively on nurturing high-profile partnerships that demand consistent attention and customized engagement. A Development Operations Manager ensures that donor data, reporting, and systems run seamlessly. These roles protect and expand the organization's most valuable revenue streams.

Ultimately, fundraising staffing must balance strategy and sustainability. Expanding too quickly can create financial strain and confusion over responsibilities, while underinvesting in development capacity leads to burnout, turnover, and missed opportunities. The most effective nonprofits reassess their fundraising structure regularly by comparing staffing to both current goals and peer benchmarks to ensure the organization has the right people, in the right roles, at the right time.

The Growth Pathway: Scaling Your Team with Intention

Just as programs evolve with demand, your fundraising team must evolve with capacity.

Each stage of growth requires new skills, systems, and structures that connect directly to your *Five Factors*™—Plan, Outcomes, Budget, Team, and Donors.

Budget Range	Core Roles	Specialized Additions	Primary Focus	Five-Factor Alignment
<$1 million	Executive Director, Development Coordinator	Volunteers, Board Fundraising Committee	Establish systems, build relationships, basic donor tracking	Plan & Team
$1–5 million	Director of Development, Major Gifts Officer, Comms/ Marketing	Annual Fund Officer, Grants Manager	Strengthen donor pipeline, diversify revenue	Plan, Budget & Donors
$5–10 million	Chief Development Officer, Operations Manager	Corporate/ Foundation Relations, Stewardship Officer	Data-driven fundraising, retention, scalable systems	Outcomes & Team
$10–50 million+	Chief Advancement Officer, Planned Giving Director	Donor Experience, Partnerships, Analytics	Strategic growth, long-term sustainability	All Five Factors™

Structure That Scales

Think of fundraising infrastructure as a living system:

- **Early growth** requires flexibility and experimentation.
- **Mid-stage growth** requires defined systems and roles.

- **Advanced growth** demands specialization and integration with finance, operations, and communications.

Each phase sets the stage for the next. The goal is not simply to "add staff," but to build a structure that sustains impact even as leadership and funding cycles change. When done right, your development department becomes a strategic engine that powers the mission forward.

Aligning Metrics with Mission

Fundraising metrics should always connect back to the organization's strategic plan. If your goal is to expand donor retention, then measure renewal rates, stewardship activities, and donor satisfaction. If you're entering a capital campaign, focus on pledged commitments, pipeline development, and long-term revenue sustainability. Metrics that reflect both financial performance and mission alignment ensure that success is defined not just by dollars raised, but by the depth and quality of relationships built.

Traditional measures, like total dollars raised or number of grants submitted, are useful but incomplete. They must be balanced with indicators that reflect the organization's values: collaboration, innovation, and community impact. The aim is to create a transparent system that helps staff understand how their work contributes to the larger mission.

From Evaluation to Accountability—Developing Key Metrics

Performance measurement in fundraising should be viewed as part of the organization's accountability framework, not an HR exercise. Clear, mission-driven metrics allow leaders to manage toward outcomes rather than activity.

Effective Metrics Balance Three Dimensions

1. **Quantitative goals**—measurable targets such as revenue raised, retention rates, or return on investment (ROI).
2. **Qualitative outcomes**—relationship-based indicators like donor satisfaction, internal collaboration, or stewardship quality.
3. **Behavioral measures**—the "how" behind performance: teamwork, innovation, strategic thinking, and alignment with organizational values.

Revenue and Efficiency Metrics

- **Funds Raised vs. Goal:** Measure progress toward campaign or annual fund targets.

- **Return on Investment (ROI):** Every dollar spent on fundraising should yield $3–$5 in revenue on average.
- **Cost-to-Dollar Raised:** Track how efficiently resources are being used to generate income.
- **Year-over-Year Growth:** Monitor trends to ensure steady, sustainable increases rather than one-time spikes.

Donor Relationship Metrics

- **Retention Rate:** The percentage of donors who give again year over year; the single most predictive indicator of long-term success.
- **New Donor Acquisition:** Track the number and value of first-time donors to ensure a healthy pipeline.
- **Donor Upgrade Rate:** Measure how many supporters increase their giving levels over time.
- **Donor Satisfaction:** Use surveys or personal feedback to gauge donor perception and trust.
- **Stewardship Activity:** Track how consistently and meaningfully donors are thanked, engaged, and informed.

Major Gift and Institutional Metrics

- **Portfolio Coverage:** For major gift officers, track the number of active prospects with personalized cultivation plans.
- **Solicitation-to-Gift Ratio:** Measure conversion rates to understand whether outreach strategies are effective.
- **Grant Success Rate:** Compare grants submitted versus awarded and analyze patterns of success.

Pipeline and Capacity Metrics

- **Prospect Pipeline Growth:** Evaluate how effectively future donors are being identified and cultivated.
- **Planned and Legacy Gifts:** Track long-term commitments that build financial sustainability.
- **Donor Churn Rate:** Identify how many donors lapse annually and why.

Collaboration and Culture Metrics

- **Cross-Department Alignment:** Assess how well development works with finance, programs, and communications.
- **Board Engagement:** Measure participation in fundraising: giving, introductions, and advocacy.
- **Innovation and Initiative:** Track implementation of new fundraising tactics, tools, or campaigns.

Example Fundraising Performance Dashboard

A well-designed fundraising dashboard gives leadership a clear snapshot of financial health, relationship strength, and organizational momentum. It helps teams focus on what truly matters, sustainable revenue and donor engagement, without getting lost in vanity metrics.

Small Nonprofit (Under $1 Million Revenue)

Category	*Metric*	*Target*	*Notes*
Revenue	Total raised vs. goal	100%+	Include grants, events, and individual giving.
Efficiency	Cost to raise $1	<$0.30	Combine direct and indirect costs.
Retention	Donor renewal rate	≥55%	Core health indicator for small orgs.
Growth	New donors added	+15% YOY	Measured through CRM or event tracking.
Engagement	Donor thank-you rate within 48 hours	100%	Use automation or templates to ensure consistency.

Mid-Size Nonprofit ($1–5 Million Revenue)

Category	*Metric*	*Target*	*Notes*
Revenue	Major gifts secured	10+ new per year	Based on capacity and prospect pipeline.
ROI	Fundraising ROI	4:1	Evaluate by channel (events, grants, annual fund).
Pipeline	Planned/legacy gifts initiated	3–5 per year	Indicates maturity and sustainability.
Retention	Major donor retention	≥ 75%	Measure both retention and upgrade rates.
Collaboration	Board participation in giving	100%	All board members should give or raise.

Large Nonprofit ($5M+ Revenue)

Category	*Metric*	*Target*	*Notes*
Revenue	Total raised vs. budget	≥105%	Include multi-year pledges and deferred gifts.
Portfolio	Active major donor prospects	100–150 per MGO	Use CRM tracking for movement through the pipeline.
Retention	Donor renewal rate	≥70%	Measured across giving tiers.
Diversity	Revenue mix	≤40% from single source	Ensures funding stability.
Culture	Staff retention	≥90%	Prevents costly turnover and protects relationships.

Dashboards should be reviewed quarterly. Over time, patterns reveal where to invest, whether in people, systems, or stewardship.

Beyond the Numbers

Metrics alone don't tell the whole story. They must be interpreted in context: how mature the organization is, how strong the donor base is, and whether the team has the right tools and training. A new program might have a lower ROI initially but be critical for long-term diversification. Similarly, donor retention could dip during a leadership transition without indicating failure.

Regular performance check-ins, either quarterly or biannual, allow leaders to spot trends early, celebrate successes, and course-correct when needed. The most effective organizations use these reviews as coaching opportunities, not compliance exercises.

Incentives That Reinforce Values

When tied to metrics, incentives should reward both outcomes and behavior. In fundraising, where relationships matter as much as revenue, the most effective systems balance quantitative goals (e.g., revenue growth, donor retention, and ROI) with qualitative outcomes (e.g., collaboration, innovation, and donor satisfaction).

This combination encourages fundraisers to pursue sustainable relationships rather than transactional wins. A balanced scorecard approach, where short-term results and long-term impact are weighted together, prevents the "chasing dollars" mentality that burns out staff and erodes donor trust.

Ethical Incentives in Fundraising

The Association of Fundraising Professionals (AFP) prohibits paying fundraisers a commission or percentage of funds raised, but it does allow performance-based bonuses tied to ethical, mission-driven criteria. These incentive systems recognize excellence while reinforcing values, teamwork, and sustainability.

Done well, bonuses serve several important functions:

- Encouraging growth and retention. Strong performers stay when they see a path for advancement.
- Aligning fundraising with organizational goals. Bonuses tied to stewardship or donor retention reinforce long-term thinking.
- Modeling professional parity with the for-profit world. Ethical incentives allow nonprofits to reward results and innovation while maintaining integrity.

Designing an Ethical Bonus Framework

Bonuses should reward measurable performance and professional conduct, not transactional fundraising. Here's an example of a balanced, values-based bonus structure:

Sample Fundraiser Scorecard

A balanced scorecard helps fundraisers and their leaders see performance through multiple lenses: revenue, relationships, innovation, and alignment with mission. The goal isn't to check boxes; it's to create a shared understanding of what success looks like and how every role contributes to long-term sustainability.

Annual Performance Scorecard

Category	*Key Metrics*	*Target/ Benchmark*	*Measurement Method*	*Weight (%)*
Financial results	- Total funds raised vs. goal - ROI of fundraising activities - Cost per dollar raised	100% of annual goal 3–5:1 ROI	Finance reports, CRM data	25

(Continued)

Category	*Key Metrics*	*Target/ Benchmark*	*Measurement Method*	*Weight (%)*
Donor retention & growth	- Donor renewal rate - Number of upgraded donors - New donor acquisition	65%+ retention 15%+ donor upgrades	CRM tracking, donor database	25
Donor experience & stewardship	- Timeliness of thank-yous - Donor satisfaction (survey or interviews) - Quality of impact reports	100% within 48 hours 90%+ donor satisfaction	Donor survey, audit of acknowledgments	20
Collaboration & leadership	- Cross-department engagement - Mentoring or training staff/ volunteers - Participation in team initiatives	Active collaboration Positive peer feedback	360 review, team check-ins	15
Innovation & professional development	- New campaign or process improvement - Continuing education (AFP, CFRE, webinars) - Contribution to strategic planning	1+ innovation implemented 10+ hours training	Leadership review, self-report	10
TOTAL SCORE	- Weighted performance across all metrics	≥85% overall = "Exceeds Expectations"	Quarterly + Annual Review	100

How to Use It

- **Set goals collaboratively.** Each metric should be discussed and agreed upon at the start of the year.
- **Review quarterly.** Identify roadblocks early, celebrate wins often, and provide support when targets are off-track.
- **Tie results to coaching and bonuses.** Use the scorecard to guide professional development and fair, mission-driven incentives.
- **Keep it transparent.** Everyone should know what "success" looks like, as this builds trust across the team and credibility with donors.

Why It Matters

A clear, balanced scorecard connects fundraising success to the organization's mission, not just its money. When fundraisers are evaluated on impact, collaboration, and sustainability, they focus on building relationships that last.

Bonuses can be paid annually or semi-annually and should be approved by leadership using pre-set criteria. Linking compensation to both values and outcomes not only boosts motivation but also helps attract top-tier development professionals who expect accountability and growth.

Incentive systems that reward integrity, collaboration, and measurable impact transform fundraising from a pressure-driven activity into a shared pursuit of excellence. When fundraisers are empowered, recognized, and supported, they elevate the entire organization.

Why the Board Matters in the Five Factors™

The board is part of the *system* that drives the organization. The balance of governance and leadership is the difference between a nonprofit that sustains itself and one that eventually crashes from burnout or poor oversight. Each of the Five Factors™ depends on an engaged and capable board:

Five Factors™	*Board's Role*
Plan	Guides vision, approves strategy, and ensures alignment between mission and long-term direction.
Outcomes	Monitors impact, demands measurable results, and ensures accountability to the public.
Budget	Oversees fiscal integrity, approves budgets, reviews audits, and ensures sustainable resource allocation.
Team	Hires, supports, and evaluates the CEO; cultivates a healthy partnership between governance and management.
Donors	Acts as ambassadors, advocates, and door-openers who strengthen credibility and expand the organization's network.

The best boards understand that they are co-pilots in mission success, not passive passengers or backseat drivers.

Building the Right Board

A strong board is intentionally built, not casually assembled. Too often, nonprofits fill seats with friends of current members or well-known names, hoping enthusiasm will substitute for structure. But effective governance requires competency, diversity, and commitment.

Start with a board matrix, identifying the skills and perspectives the organization needs to thrive: finance, legal, fundraising, marketing, lived experience, and community representation.

The matrix helps leaders recruit strategically rather than reactively, ensuring that the board reflects both the organization's values and the community it serves. Orientation should follow every appointment, just as onboarding does for staff: mission, strategy, finances, and expectations must be clearly explained from day one.

Remember, board members are unpaid, which makes recruitment even harder. They often lead thriving businesses yet step into nonprofit roles without the same discipline or accountability they demand of their own companies. That dysfunction, expecting volunteers to serve as experts, fundraisers, ambassadors, and check-writers, creates confusion and frustration. Instead, seek mission-aligned leaders who understand that governance is stewardship, not charity.

The Board as a Strategic Partner

A nonprofit's board should mirror the professionalism of a corporate board, but with deeper moral accountability. Its role is not to manage daily operations but to ensure that the organization's strategy, finances, and ethics align with mission and public trust. The board's core responsibilities fall into three interconnected domains:

1. **Strategy:** Setting and monitoring long-term goals, approving the strategic plan, and ensuring decisions serve the mission.
2. **Fiscal Oversight:** Safeguarding assets, approving budgets, reviewing audits, and ensuring sustainable financial practices.
3. **Community and Fundraising Leadership:** Acting as ambassadors, advocates, and **door-openers** who use their influence to expand visibility and resources.

When board members understand the business model and the organization's vision, they become multipliers by connecting staff to opportunities, donors, and partners who accelerate impact.

The Board as Part of the Fundraising Team

Fundraising is not just the job of the development department. It's a team sport, and the board plays a central role. Among the board's most powerful roles is that of door-opener; leveraging personal networks to connect the organization to new donors, funders, and partners. Board members make introductions, tell stories, and lend their credibility to cultivate trust. Inviting someone to a site visit, a community event, or a donor briefing often sets the stage for a gift later on.

Beyond introductions, effective board members act as champions:

- Speaking publicly about the mission.
- Sharing stories on social media.
- Hosting small gatherings or tours.
- Serving as ambassadors of integrity and impact.

When board members lead with passion and consistency, they build confidence inside and outside the organization. Their example sets the tone for staff, volunteers, and the community alike.

Just as fundraisers are trained and supported, boards need structure and accountability to fulfill this role effectively. Provide them with talking points, success stories, and data they can confidently share. Create engagement dashboards that track introductions made, events attended, and personal giving, just as you would measure other strategic metrics. When the board sees itself as a partner in development, fundraising becomes relational, not transactional.

The strongest boards are self-aware, strategic, and engaged. They understand that their power is relational and partner with leadership to set vision, secure resources, and protect the organization's reputation and mission. Strong boards hold themselves to the same standard of excellence they expect from staff.

Door-Openers vs. Check-Writers

Great boards don't just give—they grow. The most valuable board members act as door-openers, using their credibility and connections to introduce the organization to new donors, partners, and champions. Check-writers fund today; door-openers secure tomorrow.

Encourage every board member to:

- Invite one new prospect to learn about the mission each quarter.
- Share one impact story within their professional network monthly.
- Pair with staff on a donor visit at least once a year.

When board members see themselves as ambassadors, not just advisors, fundraising becomes everyone's responsibility, and the mission gains momentum.

Board Development: Planning, Assessment, and Renewal

A great board, like a great team, never stops improving. Every board should have its own business plan with goals for recruitment, education, and evaluation. Just as staff are reviewed for performance, board members should complete self-assessments that measure both individual and collective effectiveness. Questions might include:

- Do I understand the organization's mission, finances, and strategic priorities?
- Have I opened doors, contributed financially, or advocated publicly this year?
- Does our board reflect the diversity and expertise needed to govern effectively?

The assessment identifies where training, mentoring, or renewal is needed. Sometimes that means adding new skills to the board. Occasionally it means helping a member step down gracefully when their season of service has ended. When handled with transparency and care, turnover strengthens culture and keeps the board vibrant and future-focused.

Five-Factor Board Readiness Diagnostic

Rate your board on a 1–5 scale (1 = Needs significant improvement; 5 = Excellent):

Factor	*Key Indicators*	*Score (1–5)*
Plan	Board participates in setting and reviewing strategic direction.	
Outcomes	Uses metrics and dashboards to monitor impact.	
Budget	Maintains financial literacy and consistent oversight.	
Team	Partners productively with the CEO; succession plan in place.	
Donors	Members engage in giving + getting, stewardship, and advocacy.	
Average Score		

Boards, like organizations, evolve through distinct stages of maturity. Understanding where your board stands helps you identify what to strengthen next: structure, engagement, or strategic alignment. Use this scale when scoring the Five-Factor Board Readiness Diagnostic:

Emerging Board (Scores 1–2.4)

The board exists, but systems and clarity are still forming.

- **Structure:** Meetings are irregular or overly operational; roles and bylaws may not be well-defined.
- **Strategy:** Focused more on immediate issues than long-term goals; little use of data or dashboards.
- **Engagement:** A few members carry most of the weight; fundraising participation is inconsistent.
- **Culture:** Enthusiasm may be high, but accountability and shared ownership are low.
- **Next Steps:** Establish clear governance structure, role descriptions, and expectations. Begin using a board matrix and orientation plan. Prioritize recruiting for skills and diversity, not convenience.

Boards in their nascent stages frequently embody the fervor that sparked the organization's inception. The subsequent progression involves transforming this passion into a structured process.

Developing Board (Scores 2.5–3.4)

The foundation is set, but consistency and strategic focus are still growing.

- **Structure:** Regular meetings and committees are in place, but agendas often focus on updates rather than decisions.
- **Strategy:** The board reviews plans but doesn't drive or measure outcomes consistently.
- **Engagement:** Most members participate in giving, but fewer in fundraising or advocacy.
- **Culture:** Communication between the CEO and board is good but may lack regular evaluation or feedback loops.
- **Next Steps:** Strengthen committee charters, introduce performance metrics, and start using dashboards for financial and outcome monitoring. Offer training on fundraising and board roles.

Developing boards have energy and intent; now they need discipline and data.

Strategic Board (Scores 3.5–4.4)

Governance and leadership are balanced, with strong alignment around mission and metrics.

- **Structure:** Clear governance policies, active committees, and annual plans in place.
- **Strategy:** Board regularly reviews performance against goals; planning is data-informed and forward-looking.
- **Engagement:** Nearly all members give and participate in fundraising or community advocacy.
- **Culture:** Constructive partnership with the CEO; mutual accountability and respect are evident.
- **Next Steps:** Deepen board development through retreats, leadership succession planning, and external benchmarking. Expand donor and community engagement to diversify funding.

Strategic boards move from oversight to insight, shaping the future instead of reacting to it.

High-Performing Board (Scores 4.5–5.0)

Governance excellence is part of organizational DNA. The board is visionary, accountable, and fully integrated into the Five Factors™.

- **Structure:** Roles, committees, and policies operate at peak effectiveness; board refreshment and succession are routine.
- **Strategy:** Decisions are guided by long-term impact metrics and aligned with community need.
- **Engagement:** Every member is a donor, advocate, and door-opener. The board leverages networks to expand influence and resources.
- **Culture:** Transparent, collaborative, and self-reflective. Conflict is addressed constructively; learning and evaluation are ongoing.
- **Next Steps:** Mentor emerging nonprofits, publish lessons learned, and model best practices in governance, equity, and philanthropy.

High-performing boards don't just govern organizations, they grow movements.

Using the Readiness Levels

After scoring each of the Five Factors™, place your board on the continuum and ask:

1 **Where are we now?** (Be honest about the lowest-performing area.)
2 **Where do we want to be next year?** (Pick one level up as a goal.)

3 **What will it take to get there?** (Training, recruitment, new processes, or stronger partnerships.)

By visualizing progress over time, you turn board assessment into a board development plan, a living roadmap for improvement that parallels the growth of the organization itself.

Balancing Leadership: The Board–CEO Partnership

The relationship between the CEO and the board is one of the strongest predictors of nonprofit success. The CEO manages the *how*—programs, people, and execution. The board governs the *what* and *why*—mission, direction, and integrity. When both stay in their lane but move in rhythm, the organization glides forward with purpose and stability.

Leading a nonprofit is a lot like paddling a canoe. The board sits in the stern, steering toward the destination, ensuring the organization stays on course. The CEO sits in the bow, setting the pace, reading the currents, and powering the daily momentum. When both paddle in sync, the canoe moves swiftly and efficiently. When one stops paddling—or starts steering too hard—the canoe drifts off course, turns in circles, or slows to a crawl.

Balance comes from coordination, trust, and constant communication. Both leaders must stay aware of the environment, anticipate obstacles, and adjust together. If the board and CEO communicate clearly, respect each other's strengths, and share the same destination, they move faster and farther than either could alone.

Strong leadership partnership doesn't just keep the canoe afloat; it ensures the entire team reaches its destination together, mission intact and momentum strong.

Summary—The Power of the Right Team

Plans and budgets are only as strong as the people who execute them. No matter how strong a plan or mission may be, its success depends on the team that carries it out. Building a capable, motivated staff and supporting them with clear systems and healthy culture is both an HR priority and a fundraising strategy. Donors look closely at the people behind the mission, assessing leadership stability, staff competence, and organizational culture as indicators of trust and long-term viability. Investing in your team is, ultimately, an investment in credibility and impact.

Leadership and governance set the tone for everything that follows. A strong partnership between the executive director and the board creates balance and accountability. Each focusing on their respective roles in execution and oversight. Boards that are engaged, diverse, and well connected can open new opportunities for funding and visibility, while strong leadership ensures resources are managed wisely and the mission stays clear. When both work in alignment, the organization signals stability and professionalism to funders and the community.

At every level, staffing and development functions turn plans into results. Clear hiring processes, intentional onboarding, and regular professional development help ensure that employees understand their roles and can grow within the organization. In fundraising in particular, nonprofits must avoid underinvesting in development capacity. Skilled fundraisers, whether full-time or fractional, build donor relationships that sustain long-term growth. A stable, well-trained team demonstrates to donors that the organization has the infrastructure to deliver on its promises.

Finally, a strong organizational culture ties it all together. Culture shapes how people work, collaborate, and represent the mission to the public. It must reflect the organization's values, especially around fairness, inclusion, and respect. When people feel safe, supported, and valued, they stay engaged and perform better. Donors notice that too. A vibrant, equitable culture signals that the organization is disciplined, sustainable, and built to last, making it a trustworthy steward of community investment.

Key Takeaways

- People make the plan possible.
  The most effective nonprofits treat their team as their greatest asset, not a cost center. A strong team is the bridge between strategy and outcomes.
- Culture drives performance.
  A healthy, equitable culture built on respect, trust, and accountability keeps teams engaged, reduces burnout, and reinforces mission alignment.
- Leadership must stay in balance.
  The board and CEO are a team paddling a canoe, each vital to direction and stability. Strong governance and skilled management together sustain flight.
- Fundraising is a team sport.
  Success requires collaboration among leadership, finance, development, and the board. When each understands their role, donor confidence grows.
- Donors invest in competence.
  Funders look for organizations that are not only passionate but professional, and can clearly execute plans, measure results, and deliver impact.

Progress Check

After reading this chapter, rate where your organization is on a scale of one to five, with one being that your organization does not have this component, or is just beginning to work on it, and five being that your organization is fully operational and has this element ready for vetting by a major donor. Out of a maximum of 25 points, the goal is to score at least 20.

Notes:

Chapter 5

Donors—Building Partnerships That Fund the Future

This is not a book about how to fundraise. There are already plenty of excellent guides on solicitation tactics, donor psychology, and campaign mechanics. This chapter is about something more foundational: understanding *how* donors fit into the larger system of organizational sustainability.

In the Five Factors™ Framework, donors come last for a reason. The goal isn't to "get more donors" but to attract the *right* ones, essentially, people whose investments align with your plan, outcomes, budget, and team. Donors close the loop because they fund what is already working. They are the evidence of credibility, not the cause of it.

Too many organizations approach fundraising as the fix for structural problems, treating donors as the starting point rather than the sustaining force. But seasoned funders and philanthropists don't respond to desperation or volume; they respond to discipline. They look for a plan grounded in reality, a team capable of delivering, measurable outcomes that prove change, and a budget that reflects sustainability.

When those four elements are in place, even if still evolving, fundraising transforms from a scramble into an invitation. Donors no longer feel like rescuers; they feel like partners joining a credible, well-managed enterprise with a clear vision and strong return on investment.

It's also important to understand that donors don't want to be your only source of funding. In fact, most sophisticated funders see diversification as a sign of stability. They want to know their gift will leverage, and not replace, other forms of support. Anyone who has relied heavily on government contracts knows how limiting that dependence can be. Government funding may sustain basic operations, but it rarely fuels innovation or growth. Fundraising is the primary way nonprofits create margin, the flexible resources that allow organizations to move, adapt, and grow. This margin functions as the nonprofit sector's version of risk capital. It provides the breathing room to pilot new ideas, invest in infrastructure, respond to unexpected challenges, and pursue opportunities that advance the mission over time. Without

DOI: 10.4324/9781003746218-6

fundraising that intentionally builds margin, organizations are forced into a reactive posture, limited to survival rather than progress.

This chapter will help you see donors not as an unpredictable variable but as an integral part of a designed system that connects directly to your three-year plan. Here, we redefine fundraising as a relational, data-informed pipeline designed to fund long-term growth, without fragmenting efforts through competing campaigns or compromising organizational credibility.

From Campaigns to Commitment

I was recently working with a team that had been given a capital campaign goal. Leadership had handed down a number—a big, impressive number—and told them, "Go raise this much."

When I asked what portion of their annual operating needs that goal covered, the room went quiet. Someone finally said, "It doesn't." We ran the numbers together and discovered the truth: their actual need was millions higher.

Like so many nonprofits, they had been trained to think of their campaigns as separate efforts: one to keep the lights on and another to build the future. When your team divides its focus, you divide its energy. The result is predictable: you fall short on both fronts. The better path is to combine them by defining one comprehensive goal that covers both your operational and capital needs.

Your donors may give for different reasons, but your organization should have only one destination. Whether they're moved by immediate impact or long-term investment, they're all contributing to the same mission. Thus, fundraising becomes a commitment shared between your organization and your supporters to build what comes next.

The rest of this chapter explores how to design a strategy that unites your funding streams, your team, and your message. It begins by rethinking how we define and relate to donors themselves.

Rethinking Donor Segmentation

For decades, nonprofits have been taught to divide their fundraising efforts into familiar silos: grants, events, annual funds, and capital campaigns. On budget sheets, these lines become neat categories of "how" we raise money, but behind them lies a deeper truth: *how* and *who* are not the same thing.

Every organization needs to understand both. The *how* reveals the tools we use to generate revenue and do the ask: a gala, a grant proposal, or a membership drive. The *who* tells us where those funds come from: individuals, corporations, foundations, or government. However, when nonprofits build plans around these traditional categories, they often create internal competition.

The "annual fund" fights for attention against the "capital campaign." Donors are asked to choose between helping now or helping later, between sustaining today's programs or investing in tomorrow's growth. No business would operate this way, and yet the nonprofit sector has normalized it.

To change the outcome, we have to change the frame. Instead of segmenting donors by gift size or campaign type, what if we segmented them by *mindset*?

If we do this, there are really only two kinds of donors:

- **Investment-Focused Donors**, who want to help build the future. They're interested in your vision, your plan, and the systems that make long-term change possible. They want to see the Five Factors™ at work: your strategy, your measurable outcomes, your financial sustainability, your leadership, and your growth potential.
- **Present-Focused Donors**, who want to solve an immediate problem. They're motivated by urgency, clarity, and stories of impact. They want to know what they can do *right now* to make a tangible difference.

Both are vital. But too often, nonprofits speak to both types of donors with the same message, typically an emotional appeal or a crisis story, and wonder why their capital campaign stalls or why their annual fund never grows. The truth is that healthy fundraising integrates both mindsets simultaneously.

A strong fundraising system doesn't pit the "now" against the "next." It builds a strategy where immediate needs and future investments coexist. Where a donor can both feed a child today and invest in the school that ensures that child never goes hungry again.

When your plan, outcomes, budget, team, and donors are aligned, every campaign becomes part of the same story of where you're going and what it takes to get there.

From Random Appeals to a Donor Pipeline

Currently, donor engagement typically resembles scattered appeals, random social media posts, or occasional events. This leads to short-term attention but lacks lasting loyalty. A thriving organization builds intentional "channels" to guide supporters from initial curiosity to deeper connection and, ultimately, commitment. This structured approach forms the foundation of a robust donor pipeline.

In the business world, successful companies don't rely on chance; they build sales funnels that move potential customers from awareness to consideration to purchase through deliberate, measurable steps. Nonprofits can, and should, adopt this same disciplined approach to cultivating donors.

A donor pipeline replaces this chaos with structure, allowing you to view every interaction as part of a continuum: supporters first *discover* you, then *learn, trust, engage,* and finally *invest.* Just as businesses track leads from the first touch to a closed deal, your team should be able to identify where each supporter is in their journey and determine the best action to advance them to the next stage.

By thinking in these terms, fundraising becomes less about chasing individual transactions and more about managing a conversion system. Each stage of the donor journey—awareness, interest, evaluation, and commitment—becomes intentional, measurable, and repeatable.

Mapping the Donor Journey: Understanding First Contact

Every donor begins somewhere in the funnel. That first point of contact is where awareness sparks interest. In a for-profit setting, this might be an ad impression or a first website visit; for a nonprofit, it's a story shared on social media, a friend's invitation to an event, or a moving news segment about your work.

The goal is to identify and optimize these first-contact channels. Ask your team:

- Where do most new supporters first hear about us?
- Which sources convert most effectively into repeat engagement?
- Which outreach efforts attract attention but fail to build connection?

Review recent donor or volunteer data to trace the journey backward from gift to discovery. You'll begin to see patterns: what channels generate real leads, which simply build awareness, and where people drop off. This process turns instinct into insight.

> **Leadership Tip:** Schedule a team session to map your top "awareness channels." Treat this like a marketing funnel review. Discuss conversion rates, cost of acquisition, and emotional resonance. You'll begin to see where small investments could yield major relationship gains.

Designing the Journey Forward

Once you understand your entry points, your job is to guide supporters down the funnel with thoughtful, value-driven steps. The first interactions should be light and inviting: an easy sign-up, a timely thank-you, or a short impact story that reinforces why your mission matters.

As donors move deeper into the journey, your communication shifts from general awareness to personalized engagement. Instead of "please donate," the tone becomes "here's what success looks like—will you join us?" You're not rushing a sale; you're leading a relationship. You will want to emphasize positive communications that demonstrates how your organization is successfully advancing its cause. Communications that are regularly urgent and suggest the organization is in peril will not inspire confidence, nor interest in donating.

Over time, this consistent, data-driven process replaces random fundraising with a living system that attracts, nurtures, and retains support. Each digital or personal touchpoint serves a purpose in moving the donor toward partnership.

Building the System, Not the Moment

When your entire organization understands this pipeline mindset, everything changes. The receptionist greeting a visitor, the volunteer coordinator answering inquiries, or the board member sharing a post each plays a role in conversion.

Encourage your team to see themselves as part of one seamless donor experience. Use the same language for fundraising that businesses use for sales: *lead generation, conversion rate, retention, and lifetime value*. These aren't corporate buzzwords; they're accountability tools.

Hold quarterly "donor funnel reviews" to identify where prospects stall and where messaging or follow-up can be improved. This turns fundraising into a continuous improvement process rather than a series of disconnected campaigns.

When you move from random appeals to a managed pipeline, you stop guessing and start growing. Donor engagement becomes measurable, sustainable, and scalable, just like any successful business channel.

How to Use the Donor Pipeline Chart

Now it's time to map out your donor journey. The Donor Pipeline Chart is a simple but powerful tool to help visualize how relationships with donors evolve over time. This chart helps you and your team map out where each prospect or supporter flows through the relationship process, from first contact to meaningful investment, so every action moves them closer to long-term partnership in a real and authentic way.

Each column represents a distinct stage in the donor journey:

- **First Contact**—Identify how each potential donor first can connect with your organization. It may be through an event, social media, referral, or program exposure. Understanding these entry points helps you see which outreach efforts are most effective at attracting interest.
- **Follow Up**—Plan your first intentional interaction after that initial connection. A prompt thank-you note, a personalized email, or a phone

call from a board member reinforces goodwill and begins building trust. Donor databases can help you document how and when you follow up so that no contact goes unacknowledged. This is a good place to start building your database standard operating procedures.

- **Qualify**—Not every contact becomes a donor, and not every donor is a major gift prospect. Map out the process your team will use to assess interest, capacity, and alignment with your mission. Ask: Is this an annual fund donor who prefers consistent smaller gifts, or a potential investor for major or transformational giving? It is important to also know when to move a donor from one category to another: when does an annual fund donor become a major gift prospect, and when does a major gift prospect move to an annual fund donor?
- **Engage**—Move donors deeper into your mission. Invite them to volunteer, attend a site visit, host a small gathering, or join a committee. Engagement builds emotional connection and helps donors see themselves as partners, not just funders. Understand what motivates your donors.
- **Ask**—The final step is the formal request for support, but by this point, it shouldn't feel like a surprise. You've built trust, demonstrated impact, and matched their interests with your needs. Use this stage to make a clear, confident, and personalized ask that reflects the donor's journey so far.
- **Stewardship**—Once a gift has been made, stewardship ensures gratitude is expressed and impact is demonstrated. Send stories, results, and updates that show their contribution matters. This stage is where loyalty grows and the process of renewing or increasing a gift begins.

When used well, this chart becomes both a planning tool and a tracking system outline for your database. It helps staff and board members see where prospects are clustered in the pipeline, whether too many are stuck at "follow up" or if few are reaching the "engage" or "ask" stages. Regularly updating it ensures accountability, consistency, and a shared strategy across your fundraising team.

Donor Pipeline Chart

First Contact	*Follow Up*	*Qualify*	*Engage*	*Ask*	*Steward*
How do they first connect with your organization	How will you thank or follow up	How do you qualify them as major or annual fund	How can you get them deeper involved	When and how will you ask them for support	What will you to continue to say thank-you

Using Your Pipeline to Build Advocates, Not Just Donors

Your donor pipeline is a roadmap for deepening relationships and building a community of advocates. When you begin to study where people enter and how they move through your engagement process, you discover something remarkable: the act of *participation* often becomes the bridge to *philanthropy*.

In our own organization, we conducted research to better understand what inspired people to give. We analyzed every step of the donor journey to pinpoint where interest turned into commitment, where a curious observer became a true believer. What we found surprised us.

People connected with our mission in many ways, through events, referrals, social media, or volunteer days, but the moment that consistently converted interest into giving was participation in a one-hour training. Eighty percent of participants donated afterward. The training wasn't designed as a fundraising event; it was mission work. But it offered people something even more powerful: a way to understand the issue, experience the solutions, and see their role in creating change.

That realization shifted how we viewed our donor pipeline. We stopped thinking of it as a path to gifts and started seeing it as a path to *ownership*. Those trainings became the heartbeat of our engagement strategy. Each one produced not only donors but also champions who spoke about our cause with authority and conviction. Over time, our donor base transformed into a trained army of advocates who could speak our language, share our message, and expand our reach far beyond what staff alone could do.

The lesson is simple but profound: don't underestimate the power of using your core mission work to draw people closer. Donors want to do more than write checks; they want to make a difference.

Ask yourself:

- What experiences truly immerse people in your mission?
- How can you create opportunities that let them see, learn, or serve in ways that change how they think?
- Where along your donor pipeline can you offer transformation, not just information?

When you design your pipeline with mission engagement in mind, fundraising becomes the natural byproduct of shared purpose. The more people understand the *why* and the *how* behind your work, the more they want to invest in it. Every donor begins as an observer. Your job is to give them a way to participate in the story and be a part of the solution.

How People Find You—and Why That Matters

People rarely arrive through the same door. A volunteer shift can be the most persuasive experience you'll ever have to plan. A small event can make your mission tangible in a single evening. A board introduction can open a room you could not have entered alone. A short video can travel farther than you can afford to fly. Each door offers a different kind of first impression, and first impressions set expectations.

Treat those doors with care. A volunteer who gives four Saturdays has already given you something more precious than money—attention. Follow their labor with a simple debrief, a story about the outcome their time just made possible, and a clear next step. An event attendee is warmed by experience; don't let them cool for three weeks while you assemble the perfect email. A direct introduction deserves a live conversation, not a link to your website. The aim, always, is momentum. Not pressure. Momentum. You're showing them a path that makes sense, one step at a time, with a handrail of trust.

Qualification: The Gate That Protects Everyone's Time

Not everyone who loves your mission is ready to invest deeply, and not everyone who can invest deeply cares about your mission. Qualification is the gentle art of discovering where interest, capacity, and alignment intersect. It's not about exclusion; it's about fit.

Done well, qualification is an act of respect. It protects donors from asks that don't align with their priorities and protects your staff from pursuing relationships that will never truly connect. Think of it as the gate that organizes your energy: some donors belong in the annual program, where consistency and volume matter; others belong in a major gifts or investment-level journey, where depth and alignment drive success.

Unfortunately, most nonprofits skip this step. Everyone goes into the same annual fund database, with a few names pulled out when someone "seems" like a major donor. But that approach is neither efficient nor sustainable. Qualification allows you to move from guesswork to strategy. It ensures that every conversation, ask, and stewardship touchpoint matches both the donor's potential and their passion.

Using Data and Insight to Qualify

Qualification is both art and science. You start with what you *see*:

- Who responds and engages repeatedly?
- Who asks meaningful questions?
- Who gives again without being asked twice?

These behavioral signals already tell you a lot about interest and connection.

Then, you layer in data. Wealth screening and donor research tools can help you understand a donor's *capacity* to give. However, financial capacity alone doesn't tell the full story. You're not simply looking for who has money; you're identifying who has accessible, philanthropic wealth.

There's a difference between high income and available wealth. A person may earn $400,000 a year but have every dollar tied up in real estate, private school tuition, or debt. Another may have inherited stock, a family foundation, or a recent liquidity event that makes them capable of transformational giving. Wealth screening helps surface these nuances.

The CAP Framework: Capacity, Affinity, Propensity

Use the CAP model to guide qualification and prioritize relationships that are most likely to yield lasting partnership:

- **Capacity**—*Can they give?* Assess financial ability through public data, giving history, and professional background. Tools can estimate net worth, real estate holdings, and liquidity indicators, but remember, it's an estimate, not a judgment.
- **Affinity**—*Do they care?* Do they have a personal or emotional connection to your mission area? Review their past giving patterns: do they support causes like yours (education, environment, social justice, healthcare)? Someone who consistently funds the arts may not feel compelled by environmental issues, and that's okay. It's about alignment, not persuasion.
- **Propensity**—*Will they give to you?* This is the relationship dimension. How connected are they to your organization? Do they attend events, engage with your staff, volunteer, or share your content? Affinity may tell you they care about your cause. Propensity tells you they care about *your version* of it.

When you combine these three indicators, you can build a donor profile that prioritizes relationships with the highest potential for authentic connection and long-term giving.

Building a Donor Profile

Each qualified donor should have a simple, evolving profile that captures more than wealth. It should reflect their motivations, giving patterns, and relational context. Include:

- **Financial indicators:** estimated capacity, giving history, liquidity, business or real estate holdings.

- **Philanthropic focus:** primary cause areas, known grantees, past campaign support, and patterns of recurring giving.
- **Engagement level:** attendance, volunteering, committee participation, direct communication, peer connections.
- **Relational notes:** who introduced them, what inspired their interest, how they prefer to be contacted, and what outcomes they care about most.

Over time, these profiles help your organization allocate energy wisely: high-touch cultivation for those with both capacity and alignment, consistent engagement for your annual donors, and mission-based education for emerging supporters.

Qualification as a Culture, Not a Step

When your organization builds qualification into its culture, donor relationships become more intentional, respectful, and sustainable. You're no longer "fishing" for big gifts; you're curating partnerships based on shared values and mutual capacity.

This discipline also improves equity and professionalism. It ensures that asks are made thoughtfully, not based on assumptions about someone's neighborhood, last name, or title. It moves fundraising from intuition to intelligence. Qualification is not about who *belongs*; it's about who's *ready*. The goal is to match generosity with mission in a way that honors both the donor's goals and your organization's purpose.

When you qualify donors well, you strengthen trust, steward time wisely, and create a pipeline built not on chance, but on clarity.

Two Paths, One Stream: Navigating Annual Fund and Major Gifts

Think of your fundraising not as two disconnected programs, but as one continuous stream. Every donor begins in the same current, drawn by curiosity, moved by mission, and carried forward by meaningful engagement. As the relationship develops, the stream naturally divides into two channels: one broad and steady, the other narrower and deeper. Both are vital to your ecosystem.

The Broad Channel: Annual Fund

The annual fund is the wide, steady flow that keeps your organization alive and healthy. It's where most donors begin, and where many happily remain. This current moves through familiar channels: emails, letters, social media, events, and updates that maintain connection and build consistency.

Its rhythm is inclusive and collective: many hands, steady cadence, clear impact. You're communicating with a larger audience, providing shared stories of progress, and making it easy for donors to see that their ongoing gifts keep the mission in motion. Annual fund giving turns belief into habit.

The Deep Channel: Major Gifts

As the current flows, some donors begin to move into deeper water. They ask different questions. They want to understand the arc of your next three years, what it costs to achieve the outcomes you've promised, and how they can play a role beyond a single gift. These donors aren't responding to appeals; rather they're joining your strategy.

Major gifts flow from relationships built through careful qualification. Once you've identified capacity, affinity, and propensity, your engagement becomes more personalized. Rather than newsletters, they receive tailored updates. Instead of a general tour, they're invited to a private briefing. Instead of one-time appeals, they discuss long-term goals, risk, and measurable outcomes. These donors are co-authoring the work. Treat them as collaborators who will stay because they can see their fingerprints on the results.

Where Qualification Shapes the Flow

Qualification is what determines when the stream divides. It's not about separating donors by worth, but by *fit*. Using wealth screening, giving histories, and personal observation, you identify who is best served by the annual fund's collective communication and who needs a more customized, relational approach.

- **Annual Fund Donors:** Many donors with broad interests and moderate capacity. They thrive on shared stories, consistent updates, and efficient communication.
- **Major Gift Donors:** Fewer donors with higher capacity and deeper mission alignment. They respond to personalized engagement, strategy discussions, and direct involvement.

One Mission, Two Currents

The annual fund and major gifts are not two separate activities; they're two parts of the same current that must stay in sync. Donors may move between them fluidly: a first-time giver who begins with a small monthly gift may later invest in a major initiative; a major donor may later prefer to sustain through recurring support.

Your job is to keep the currents coordinated, ensuring the language, story, and data align across both experiences. The message is consistent: *This is one mission, powered by many forms of generosity.* The annual fund is the current that sustains you. Major gifts are the deeper channel that propels you forward. The strength of your fundraising depends not on how different they are, but on how seamlessly they flow together.

Segmentation and Timing: Different Currents, Different Conversations

In your donor pipeline, every supporter moves at a different pace. Knowing where they are in that journey shapes the ask. This is why segmentation, distinguishing between annual fund donors and major or transformational investors, is critical to both donor experience and organizational sustainability.

For annual fund donors, the ask is woven into a rhythm of consistent connection. These donors give year after year, often in smaller amounts, because they believe in your mission and trust your stewardship. Their engagement is fueled by shared stories and regular reminders of progress. The ask might take the form of:

- Email campaigns or direct mail appeals
- Social media calls to action
- Peer-to-peer fundraisers or crowdfunding challenges
- Annual events like a breakfast, gala, or giving day

The tone for these asks is inclusive and collective: "Together, we make this possible."

By contrast, major and transformational donors require a more deliberate and individualized approach. Their journey moves more slowly but with greater potential impact. These donors are not responding to broad appeals. They are choosing to invest strategically in the outcomes that matter to them. Cultivation may take 12–18 months or longer, and it must be guided by trust, transparency, and shared purpose.

Major gift donors need to be:

- Engaged in planning—Invite them into the conversation early. Remember the rule: *ask for advice before you ask for money.*
- Cultivated with evidence—Share measurable outcomes, impact reports, and ROI data that demonstrate you deliver results.
- Connected personally—Through briefings, coffee meetings, and private tours that show them how their investment changes lives.

Transformational gifts are typically multi-year commitments designed to advance your strategic plan, expand programs, or build long-term capacity.

They are not one-time acts of generosity. They are sustained partnerships in solving a problem.

Explaining Areas of Philanthropic Value

Before you can make a compelling ask, you must define what you're inviting donors to invest in. These are your Areas of Philanthropic Value, the distinct parts of your mission where meaningful change happens and where donors can see themselves making a tangible difference.

When you review your organizational plan, identify two to four specific areas that can become investment opportunities. For example, a school might focus on technology and innovation, but also on emotional intelligence and global citizenship. Some donors will resonate with preparing students for the future of work; others will be moved by the goal of raising compassionate, culturally aware leaders.

Defining these areas gives shape to your story. It allows donors to connect their personal values and philanthropic goals with your organization's real-world impact. Instead of a general appeal for support, you can show exactly *how* their investment fuels the change they care about most. Create simple one-page summaries of each Area of Philanthropic Value, including a short description, measurable outcomes, and the investment needed to achieve them. These will later become part of your pitch deck.

Putting It All Together: The Pitch Deck

Once your plan, outcomes, budget, team, and donor strategy are in place, the next step is to pull everything together into a Pitch Deck, a concise, visual, and narrative tool that captures your organization's vision and investment opportunity.

At Sharity, we use this process with all of our clients. It's one of the most transformative tools we've introduced to the nonprofit sector because it changes the way organizations talk about themselves, from *fundraising* to *investment readiness*. The concept evolved from entrepreneurship courses and accelerator programs that teach founders how to approach venture capitalists. We adapted those same principles for nonprofit use: clarity, confidence, and a focus on value creation.

Just as a startup founder pitches an investor, a nonprofit leader must be able to articulate:

- The problem being solved
- The solution and how it works
- The measurable outcomes
- The investment needed
- The expected social return

This approach helps nonprofits speak in the language of strategy and results. A well-designed pitch deck can also serve as the foundation for all of your funding materials. Your grants, prospectuses, campaign proposals, and donor briefings can all grow from the same structure. Once your message and visuals are unified, every version, from a two-minute elevator pitch to a 20-slide board presentation, stays consistent and aligned. And unlike a printed case statement, a pitch deck is not static. It should evolve over time. Each presentation is an opportunity to test and refine your story:

- Add slides when donors ask new questions.
- Remove what doesn't resonate.
- Tailor the deck for different audiences: new prospects, long-time supporters, corporate partners, or foundations.
- Keep a "core deck" that holds your essentials, then build modular slides around it to customize.

When you start to think of your pitch deck as a *living, learning document*, you'll discover how versatile it can be. It becomes both your messaging lab and your master tool, one that merges every element of your Five Factors™ Framework into a single, coherent story:

- Plan: Why your organization exists and where it's going.
- Outcomes: What change you create and how you measure success.
- Budget: What it costs to deliver that change.
- Team: Who is leading the charge.
- Donors: How partners can join and what their investment will make possible.

Building the Deck

Your deck should answer the core questions that every thoughtful donor or investor asks:

1 Why was your organization founded? What spark or injustice inspired it?
2 What societal problem are you addressing, and why now?
3 How are you solving it, and what is your theory of change?
4 What are your measurable outcomes? (Show data, not just emotion.)
5 What does success cost? Lay out the investment for the next two to three years.
6 How will you use those funds? These are your *Areas of Philanthropic Value*.
7 What secured revenue already exists? (grants, earned income, or pledges).

8 Who else is involved? Partners, early donors, or community champions.
9 What are you asking this donor to invest in specifically?
10 How will you recognize or engage them in the process?

Your pitch deck enhances relationship building. It allows you to present your vision visually and strategically, anchoring the conversation in shared understanding and measurable impact. The best pitch decks don't "sell" the mission; they invite donors to *co-own* the solution. When used well, it becomes the single, adaptable tool that ties together every ask your organization will make.

The Pitch, Once the Groundwork Is Real

When Plan, Outcomes, Budget, and Team are present, your pitch can be as short as an elevator or as long as a boardroom. You start with the change you are pursuing and why now is the moment. You show the method and how you'll know it works. You reveal the three-year investment and the portion already in hand. You offer clear areas of philanthropic value and name who's already with you, not to brag, but to signal shared confidence. And then you ask, plainly and respectfully, for a commitment that matches the role they want to play.

Stewardship That Builds Retention

Now that you have brought in that gift, no matter what the size, a thank-you is necessary, Stewardship is transformative. It's what turns a first-time gift into a lifelong investment of time, resources, and influence. Fundraisers often underestimate its power. Stewardship is not an afterthought or an administrative task; it is the single greatest driver of donor retention.

Today's donors expect more than appreciation; they expect evidence. Outcome minded supporters want to see motion in the numbers and meaning in the stories. That doesn't mean drowning them in dashboards; it means showing them how their gift made something happen.

If they helped launch a workforce program, show graduation, placement, and retention rates, and tell the story of the first family to cross a threshold because of it. Share wins and lessons learned with equal candor. Nothing builds confidence like honest learning in public.

However, safety should always be prioritized for organizations dealing with sensitive issues: domestic violence, recovery, mental health. Replace tours with private mission briefings or anonymized composites. Use third-party validations and cohort-level data to demonstrate effectiveness. Train your entire team, including your board, on what can be shared and what must remain confidential.

The Donor Stewardship Matrix: Making Stewardship Systemic

Stewardship should be intentional, not incidental. The Donor Stewardship Matrix provides a comprehensive framework for managing donor recognition, reporting, and relationship building across your organization. It ensures that stewardship is built into the process, so no donor is forgotten and no thank-you delayed.

The matrix outlines *who* is responsible for each action, *when* it should happen, and *how* acknowledgments are delivered. It helps your team provide consistent, timely, and appropriate engagement for every donor, regardless of gift size or staff turnover. By institutionalizing stewardship, you create a rhythm of appreciation that strengthens retention and builds long-term trust.

Timeliness is one of the most important aspects of stewardship. A delayed thank-you signals indifference and erodes confidence. Whether it's a first-time gift or a multi-year pledge, every donor should feel that their contribution was seen, valued, and acted upon immediately. Acknowledging a gift within 24–48 hours, either by note, email, or phone call, communicates gratitude and competence in equal measure.

The following matrix maps who receives what touchpoints, how often, and from whom. For example:

- **Annual Fund Donors:** automated thank-you emails within 24 hours, quarterly impact newsletters, an annual appreciation video, and inclusion in year-end celebration communications.
- **Mid-Level Donors:** handwritten thank-you notes, semi-annual mission updates, personalized invitations to events, and an optional program briefing once per year.
- **Major Donors:** immediate personal thank-you from leadership, quarterly impact briefings, custom reports showing ROI and outcomes, and invitations to small-group donor strategy sessions.

Consistency is what earns trust, and automation ensures no one is missed. Build your Stewardship Matrix directly into your CRM system so that reminders, templates, and next steps are triggered automatically. This turns stewardship from a personality-driven act into a replicable process that lives beyond any single staff member.

Think of this template as a starting point. Customize it to fit your organization's size, capacity, and culture. Review it annually. Donor expectations evolve, and so should your follow-up strategy. Use surveys, one-on-one feedback, and retention data to refine your approach.

The goal is not just to thank donors, but to create a systematic rhythm of appreciation, transparency, and accountability that keeps them engaged and inspired. Stewardship done well doesn't just recognize generosity, it sustains it.

				Fist Time Donors	*Recurring Donors*	*Mid-level*	*Major*	*Capital*	*Planned Gift*
Donor Stewardship Matrix									
	Stewardship/Action Item	*Timeline*	*Team member*						
Acknowledgment	Email	24 hours							
	Letter	48 hours							
	Handwritten note	1 week							
	Call	48 hours							
Recognition	Fundraiser	Annual							
	Newsletter	Monthly							
	Social	Monthly							
	Gift/Plaque	One time							
	Press release	One time							
Reporting	Annual report	Annual							
	Website	Annual							

(Continued)

				Fist Time Donors	*Recurring Donors*	*Mid-level*	*Major*	*Capital*	*Planned Gift*
Donor Stewardship Matrix									
	Stewardship/Action Item	*Timeline*	*Team member*						
Stewardship	VIP Event	Quarterly							
	Volunteer	Monthly							
	Corporate team building	Quarterly							
	Birthday	Annual							
	Holiday	Annual							
	Anniversary	Annual							
	Video	Annual							
	Thank a thon	Annual							
	CEO lunch	Annual							
	Tour	Monthly							

Where to Spend Your Energy

It's tempting to chase every lapsed donor and mourn every quiet one. Resist. The better investment is to grow the middle and protect the top.

- Mid-level donors, faithful, sometimes overlooked, respond beautifully to being seen. Give them named programs, short briefings, and one practical way to stretch: a matched upgrade, a monthly option, or a visit to see the work.
- Top supporters deserve personalization in everything: updates, recognition, and opportunities to bring others along. You're honoring the infrastructure that makes impact possible.

Reactivation has its place, but only when there's a genuine reason to reconnect: a new strategy, a problem solved, or a trusted voice making the introduction. Otherwise, accept that silence is also information and invest where momentum lives.

Balancing Time and Investment Flow

In major gifts fundraising, each donor represents a different level of investment—of both your time and their potential giving. Think of your donor strategy as a river system. The flow must be steady and intentional—with each tributary (donor stream) feeding the greater current of organizational growth. If too much energy pools in one area, the current slows; balance keeps the system alive and moving.

Review your caseload quarterly. Reallocate energy where the flow strengthens—donors moving downstream toward greater commitment. When tributaries run dry, redirect the current to new sources of potential. The goal is to keep the river of generosity in motion.

Donor	*Caseload Share*	*Time Allocation*	*Strategy Focus*	*Typical Outcomes*
Major	10–15% of portfolio	50% of your time	Deeply personal—custom engagement, direct dialogue, and tailored asks	Transformational investments (six- or seven-figure gifts), long-term partnerships
Mid-level	40–50% of portfolio	30% of your time	Targeted—intentional touchpoints blending personal outreach and structured communication	Significant gifts (five-figure range), retention, and consistent upgrades

(Continued)

Donor	*Caseload Share*	*Time Allocation*	*Strategy Focus*	*Typical Outcomes*
Present focused	50–65% of donor base	20% of your time	Broad flow—efficient, scalable engagement through events, updates, and recognition	Renewals, modest upgrades, early cultivation for future potential

After the Event: Stewardship That Starts the Next Conversation

Events, whether online or in person, are not the finish line; they are the opening of a new relationship. Yet most nonprofits treat events as a one-day success instead of a step in the donor pipeline. After investing weeks planning, promoting, and hosting, they often make the mistake of going silent until the next invitation goes out.

Every person who attends an event has already said "yes" once. They've given their time, attention, and curiosity. The event itself is just the first handshake. What you do next determines whether that interest grows into partnership or fades into memory.

Immediately after each event, take time to qualify and route attendees into the appropriate donor flow:

- Warm prospects are those who asked questions, signed up for more information, or connected emotionally, and should enter your engagement or cultivation path. Schedule a follow-up call, invitation, or update within a week.
- Active donors or sponsors belong in your stewardship path, receiving a timely thank-you, event highlights, and a clear note about what their participation made possible.
- First-time attendees should receive a personalized follow-up within 48 hours. A simple message like, "We're so glad you joined us. Here's one story your participation supports," bridges the event experience to your mission outcomes.

Treat every event as a qualification tool, not a transaction. Ask: *Who leaned in? Who gave feedback? Who seemed genuinely moved?* Then move those names into your CRM, tag them appropriately, and assign next steps. The goal is not to chase every attendee, but to identify the ones ready for a deeper relationship.

Common Pitfalls and How to Avoid Them

The most common stewardship failures aren't about effort; they're about alignment.

- Running two competing capital and annual campaigns and blaming "donor fatigue."
- Mistaking activity for progress: lots of posts, few relationships.
- Romanticizing storytelling while neglecting outcomes: moving hearts but not commitments.

The solutions are straightforward:

- One comprehensive case for support.
- One coordinated calendar.
- One CRM system tracking every touch.

Stewardship is not about the number of thank-yous you send; rather it's about how well each one reinforces trust, connection, and results. When you systematize it, your organization stops chasing new donors and starts keeping the ones you've already inspired. That's where sustainability and genuine growth begin. Retention isn't luck. It's earned, structured, and measured. Stewardship is the process that proves outcomes and turns belief into partnership.

Bless and Release: Respectful Endings Build Stronger Reputations

Not everyone who attends, donates, or interacts with your organization will want to continue the relationship, and that's okay. One of the healthiest practices in fundraising is knowing when to bless and release.

If a person consistently declines invitations, never responds to follow-ups, or simply says, "I'm not interested," take them at their word. Thank them genuinely for their past engagement and release them from ongoing solicitations. This shows professionalism, maturity, and respect for the donor's autonomy.

That doesn't mean erasing them completely. You can:

- Keep them on your annual impact mailing or newsletter if they've agreed to stay informed.
- Offer the option to remain a "Friend of the Organization," receiving updates but no asks.

- Provide an easy, positive way to opt out without guilt—"We'd love to keep you informed, but only if it's valuable to you."

This practice protects your reputation and your team's energy. It ensures your communications are focused on those who want to hear from you, not wasted on those who don't. It also leaves the door open. Many donors reengage years later, remembering that you honored their boundaries. Stewardship is about respect, not persistence. Know when to pursue and when to gracefully let go. Saying thank-you and moving on with gratitude is one of the most powerful forms of professionalism your organization can model.

Understanding Annual Funds, Campaigns, and the Power of a Comprehensive Approach

Understanding the difference between an annual fund and a campaign is essential to building a financially sustainable organization, but just as important is understanding how both depend on a strong, multi-year budget. A well-built three-year budget doesn't just tell you what you need to operate; it becomes the roadmap for what you need to raise.

Most nonprofits view their annual fund as the steady heartbeat of the organization, providing unrestricted, recurring support for programs, staff, and daily operations. It's what keeps the lights on, the doors open, and the mission moving forward. Annual funds are typically composed of smaller, repeatable gifts through membership drives, online giving, direct mail, peer-to-peer efforts, and community events. The goal is participation and consistency.

Campaigns, by contrast, are focused, time-bound fundraising efforts for a specific purpose: constructing a building, launching a major initiative, expanding programs, or building an endowment. They rely heavily on major gifts, foundation support, and corporate partnerships. The tactics differ: annual funds build reliability through rhythm; campaigns build capacity through focus.

Problems arise when organizations treat these as separate efforts. Many nonprofits run both simultaneously: two calendars, two committees, and two sets of messaging, which forces staff and donors into a constant state of competition. Instead of reinforcing one another, these campaigns fragment attention, dilute impact, and exhaust both the organization and its supporters.

The solution is not to choose between them, but to integrate them. A comprehensive campaign unites both streams under one coherent, data-driven story. It funds the entire picture—operations, growth, and capital—so your organization can sustain what's working while building for what's next.

Building a Comprehensive Campaign: From Budget to Goal

If you've completed the budget chapter, you already have the foundation in place. You've built a clear three-year operating and growth budget that reflects your real costs, realistic revenue, and planned expansion. Now, that same document becomes the backbone of your comprehensive campaign plan. The financial roadmap that shows donors exactly what it will take to bring your mission to life.

Step One: Define Your Total Campaign Goal

With your plan and budget complete, determining your campaign goal is straightforward. The goal is the sum of what it will actually take to deliver your mission over the next three years.

Start with your three-year budget you've already developed earlier in this book. It should include:

- All operating expenses (programs, salaries, benefits, rent, insurance, technology, communications, and fundraising)
- Projected growth costs (new programs, expanded staffing, or pilot initiatives)
- Capital investments (renovations, new facilities, major equipment, or technology upgrades)

Then bring those numbers together:

Budget Total Year 1 + Budget Total Year 2 + Budget Total Year 3 = Comprehensive Campaign Goal

This step creates clarity and credibility. It moves your fundraising strategy from aspiration to evidence. When your campaign goal reflects your actual costs, it becomes a comprehensive campaign, not a capital one. Donors can see the full picture: what it takes to sustain the present, grow responsibly, and build the infrastructure that ensures long-term success.

Transparent, data-driven numbers inspire confidence. Sophisticated donors, like institutional funders, want to see that your ask is based on financial discipline, not desperation. You're not asking for "more funding"; you're showing what it takes to execute your plan and deliver measurable outcomes.

Once you've calculated your total cost, determine your philanthropic gap, the portion that must be raised through private giving.

Step Two: Identify Reliable Revenue

Next, identify your most stable, predictable sources of income with 80% confidence. This includes earned revenue, government contracts, multi-year grants, pledged gifts, and consistent annual donations. Add these together to determine your confirmed revenue base:

Revenue Year 1 + Revenue Year 2 + Revenue Year 3 = Estimated Campaign Revenue

When you show donors both what you need and what's already secured, you give them a reason to believe. You're not saying, "We hope to get there." You're showing, "We're already more than halfway there." That confidence shifts the donor conversation from scarcity to momentum, an invitation to complete something that's already succeeding.

Step Three: Calculate the Philanthropic Gap

Subtract your reliable revenue from your total campaign goal. The remainder represents your fundraising target, the amount to be raised through private donations, corporate gifts, and foundation support.

Campaign Goal – Estimated Campaign Revenue = Campaign Fundraising Goal

When expressed visually, this becomes a powerful communication tool. For example, a $12 million campaign over three years might feel ambitious. But if $6 million is already secured through earned revenue, grants, and pledged gifts, you're already 50% to goal before you even launch. Donors see progress, not pressure. They're drawn to momentum, not need.

Consider this example

An organization needs to raise $4 million to construct a new education building. Over the next three years, their total operating budget will be $5 million, for a total campaign need of $9 million.

$4M (Building) + $5M (Operating) = $9M Campaign Goal

They know they will generate $2 million through program fees and another $3 million through annual giving and pledged gifts.

$2M (Earned Revenue) + $3M (Annual Fund/Pledges) = $5M Estimated Campaign Revenue

Subtracting the $5 million in reliable revenue leaves $4 million to be raised through philanthropy.

$9M (Goal) – $5M (Secured) = $4M Philanthropic Target

That means they are already 56% to goal before launching the campaign. Showing donors that kind of progress immediately positions the organization as credible and ready for investment.

Why Comprehensive Beats Capital

Traditional fundraising advice once warned that capital campaigns "steal" from annual funds, forcing donors to choose between keeping the lights on or funding the dream project. But that's outdated thinking. When structured comprehensively, these efforts reinforce one another. The annual fund sustains today while the campaign builds tomorrow.

Your three-year budget aligns everything under one story that tells donors: "Here's what it takes to run our organization well, grow responsibly, and build the infrastructure that makes it all possible."

This clarity lets you segment donors by motivation, not by arbitrary labels. Some will resonate with operational stability, others with long-term transformation. Both belong to the same vision, and both are essential to funding the full mission.

To achieve this, you must have all Five Factors™ in place: a strong Plan, measurable Outcomes, a sustainable Budget, a capable Team, and engaged Donors. Without these elements, you cannot cultivate investment-level giving. When they align, your campaign becomes a statement of readiness. You're inviting investment in a mission that's proven, planned, and ready to scale.

The Three-Year Picture

A comprehensive campaign is like a three-year pro forma, a complete financial model that unites operations, growth, and capital under one transparent case. It prices what it costs to sustain what works, fix what doesn't, and add what's needed to expand impact.

When you map what's already covered and what still needs funding, your campaign narrative writes itself. Everyone works from the same roadmap. Staff see focus instead of confusion. Donors see credibility instead of chaos. And your board can stand before the community with conviction, saying:

> This isn't a wish list. It's our next three years—fully costed, strategically prioritized, and ready to deliver measurable results.

Where to Find Donors: Expanding the Circles

Now that you have your campaign goal and a pitch deck, where do we find the donors to fund our plan? Finding new donors is about widening the ripples that already exist around your organization. Imagine your donor network as a series of concentric circles expanding outward across the surface of a pond. The first drop of water, your mission, your impact, creates waves that move farther only when the center is strong.

Start at the Center: The Inner Circle

The innermost circle holds those who already believe, such as your board members, staff, volunteers, and long-time supporters. These individuals are emotionally invested and can become your most powerful advocates and early investors. Begin with them. Share your pitch deck, test your messaging, and refine your story based on their feedback. When they invest first, it signals credibility to others.

Donors often take cues from insiders: if your own leadership and volunteers are giving, it reassures outside prospects that your mission is sound and your management trustworthy. Early gifts from your inner circle serve as the momentum that starts the ripple.

Why the Board Must Be "First In"

Every successful campaign begins with the board. Before you seek a single outside gift, your board must demonstrate full belief in the mission by giving 100%. Donors look to the board as the ultimate signal of confidence. If those closest to the organization won't invest, why should anyone else?

A board's participation isn't about the size of the gift; it's about the strength of commitment. Each member should give at a level that is personally meaningful and proportionate to their capacity. Collectively, their early support sends a powerful message that the organization is unified, credible, and ready for outside investment. When a board hesitates to give, it's a red flag. If insiders are uncertain or disengaged, outsiders will interpret that as doubt in the leadership or mission.

Second Circle: Strengthen What You Already Have

Before you move outward, evaluate the resources you already hold. Your current donor database is a gold mine of untapped potential. Use wealth screening tools to analyze capacity, affinity, and giving history. You may find that a loyal $500 donor actually has the capacity to give $50,000 but was never asked.

Develop a cultivation strategy around what you learn. Segment donors by engagement and potential. Strengthen relationships with those most aligned to your mission before you begin cold outreach. It's almost always easier and more sustainable to deepen existing relationships than to start from scratch.

Third Circle: Asset Mapping

Once your base is strong, begin identifying new relationships through asset mapping, a process that helps you uncover the people, institutions, and businesses already connected to your network.

Invite your board, staff, and volunteers to map their connections across three key areas:

- Personal relationships: family, friends, and acquaintances who might share your values.
- Professional networks: colleagues, vendors, and business partners who respect your work.
- Community and institutional ties: foundations, civic groups, and corporate sponsors with overlapping missions.

Be transparent about how you'll use the information and ensure confidentiality. When done ethically, asset mapping turns social capital into strategic capital, helping your team discover warm leads instead of relying on cold lists. Once you've compiled these connections, research and prioritize them. Focus on shared values, interests, and giving patterns before you reach out.

Fourth Circle: The Listening Tour

Large campaign firms often call this process a *feasibility study*, but a listening tour is far more authentic and far more effective when you lead it yourself. A listening tour is a structured outreach effort where you share your draft strategic or campaign plan with key community members, influencers, and potential donors to gather feedback, surface insights, and build genuine buy-in.

The goal is to raise perspective. When people feel their voices helped shape your direction, they become emotionally invested in your success. A simple opening can set the tone:

> We're meeting with community leaders to gather input on our vision for the future. Your perspective will help us refine our plans before we bring them to our board and broader community.

This approach lowers defenses and opens doors that might otherwise stay closed. People love being asked for advice. It signals respect for their expertise. These conversations often reveal unexpected allies, connectors, or champions who might never have emerged through a traditional fundraising approach.

During your listening tour, ask open-ended, conversational questions such as:

- "What do you think of our approach so far?"
- "Who else do you think we should be talking to?"
- "What challenges do you see ahead, and how might we navigate them?"

Record both *what* people say and *how* they say it. Are they enthusiastic? Skeptical? Connected? Influential? These impressions will help you identify future campaign leaders, ambassadors, and advocates. Once all interviews are complete, compile a short report summarizing the key themes, opportunities, and areas for refinement. Then share that feedback internally and, where appropriate, with your stakeholders to demonstrate transparency and collaboration. When donors see that their input shaped your final plan, they feel a sense of ownership that no consultant-led process can replicate.

After the listening tour, continue the "advice-first" approach with select prospects. Reach out with a message such as:

> We're seeking information and insight, not funding at this stage. We'd love your perspective on our plan as we refine our strategy.

This simple phrase lowers barriers and keeps conversations relational rather than transactional. It also helps you gauge a prospect's interest, influence, and alignment long before a formal ask. Done well, the listening tour doesn't just collect data, it builds trust, strengthens relationships, and transforms potential donors into invested partners in your mission.

Feasibility Studies—What You Need to Know before Writing the Check

After completing your listening tour, someone on your board will inevitably ask, "Shouldn't we do a feasibility study?" It's a fair question, but before you write that check, you should understand what you're buying, what you're giving up, and what you can easily do yourself.

Most feasibility studies are expensive and unnecessary. Hiring a campaign firm for this step can cost $30,000–$75,000 or more, plus $5,000–$8,000 in travel and expenses. If the firm recommends moving forward, you'll also need $150,000–$250,000 in cash to cover consulting fees before any campaign dollars begin arriving. Since campaign revenue often takes six to nine months to materialize (and is often restricted), the financial burden lands squarely on your operations long before the first gift is received.

The truth is, you can do this work yourself and do it better. A feasibility study is simply a structured way to test whether your campaign is viable. You already have the tools to do that through your Five Factors™ Framework: a strong plan, measurable outcomes, a realistic budget, a capable team, and a base of donors who believe in you. If those elements are in place, you're ready to test your readiness through relationships, not consultants.

Here's the reality of what your board needs to know:

- **Feasibility studies don't create donors; they measure readiness.**
  Consultants don't bring wealthy investors with them. Donors give to organizations they trust, not firms they've never met.
- **Most studies tell you what your network already knows.**
  If you've done a listening tour and gathered honest feedback, you already have the insights you'd pay a consultant to summarize.
- **The "no-go" recommendation is common—and costly.**
  Many firms conclude that organizations aren't ready for a campaign, then suggest another paid study once "issues are addressed." That cycle drains both resources and goodwill.
- **Donors prefer hearing from you.**
  Being interviewed by a consultant can feel transactional. When you lead the conversations yourself, it deepens trust and builds the relationships you'll need when you eventually ask for support.

The better path is simple: turn your listening tour into your feasibility process. Share your draft plan, test your pitch deck, ask for feedback, and refine your message. Those conversations yield the same insights a formal study would, without the cost and without the distance a third party introduces.

If you lack internal experience or confidence, consider hiring a coach instead of a full campaign firm. A good coach can help shape your materials, guide donor conversations, and strengthen your internal systems for a fraction of the price. Don't buy validation you can build yourself. A feasibility study isn't proof of readiness; it's confirmation of what strong planning and authentic relationships already reveal. Use your resources to grow capacity, not consultants.

The "Last-In" Donor: The Finisher Who Seals the Vision

As your campaign gains traction, a specific type of donor often emerges: the "last-in" investor. These donors aren't hesitant; they're strategic. They want to see proof of momentum before they commit. For them, giving at the end of a campaign is about validation. Their contribution serves as the final vote of confidence that brings the project to life.

"Last-in" donors are often seasoned philanthropists or corporate funders who understand risk. They want assurance that others have already invested, that your organization has demonstrated competence, and that the finish line is within reach. They take satisfaction in closing the gap with the gift that completes the vision and ensures success.

These donors are especially drawn to challenge or matching gifts because they multiply impact and inspire urgency. A well-structured match can turn their desire to be the finisher into a motivational tool that galvanizes your entire donor base.

To cultivate and engage these donors effectively:

- **Track and communicate progress clearly.** Show what's been raised, what remains, and who has already stepped up. Transparency builds trust.
- **Frame their role as catalytic, not supplementary.** Last-in donors want to *seal the deal,* not fill a hole. Make it clear their support will push the project over the line and unlock its full potential.
- **Stay in touch during the campaign.** They may not give early, but they're paying attention. Keep them informed through personalized updates that show growing momentum and credibility.
- **Time your ask carefully.** The best moment to approach is when you're 75–85% toward your goal and can confidently show that success is inevitable with their partnership.

"Last-in" donors remind us that every campaign has phases and every donor plays a different role. Some lead with vision, some sustain with faith, and others finish with flourish. Steward each with equal respect, but recognize that finishing strong often depends on the ones who wait to give last, not least.

Donor discovery isn't about fishing randomly. Start close, strengthen your base, and expand outward with intention. Use your CRM to document each stage: inner-circle commitments, wealth-screened upgrades, mapped assets, listening-tour prospects, and final "closers."

The Power of Authentic Moments

If you've been in the nonprofit world long enough, you've probably experienced a moment that no campaign or script could ever create. You're giving a tour, and a client says something so profound it brings everyone to tears. A child runs up to a donor, proudly showing the artwork they made in your program. A fish surfaces in a once-dead stream just as you're describing the impact of your restoration work. In those small, unplanned moments, something extraordinary happens, the connection becomes real.

These are the moments donors remember years later. They're not about polished presentations or carefully staged outcomes; they're about authenticity, truth, and emotion aligning in a way that no marketing plan can replicate. They remind donors, and us, why the work matters.

Authenticity isn't a tactic; it's a reflection of organizational integrity. Donors are incredibly good at sensing when something feels rehearsed or transactional. They're not looking to be sold a story, they want to *feel* the story. When leaders and staff show up as real people, sharing genuine passion, uncertainty, and gratitude, they invite donors into a relationship built on trust.

That doesn't mean leaving these experiences entirely to chance. It means creating environments where authenticity can surface naturally. Instead of manufacturing emotion, you prepare the conditions for it:

- Invite donors into real spaces where the work happens, where the impact lives. Let them see the people, places, and progress for themselves.
- Empower staff and clients to speak in their own voices, not through talking points. Their lived experiences carry more power than any brochure.
- Train your team to observe, not orchestrate. The goal isn't to "stage" impact, but to notice it when it occurs and hold space for it.
- Follow up authentically. After those moments, send a personal note, a candid photo, or a reflection that honors what was shared.

Authenticity also applies to vulnerability. It's okay to admit the work is hard, messy, and ongoing. In fact, donors appreciate honesty far more than perfection. When they see that your organization values transparency over performance, it deepens their sense of partnership.

Ethical and Trauma-Informed Donor Engagement: Protecting and Honoring Clients

As we think about deepening donor engagement, it's essential to remember that transparency should never come at the expense of dignity. The people we serve are not exhibits in our success, they are partners in the work.

Years ago, during a donor tour, a client quietly told me she often felt like she was "in a zoo" when people came through to see the work. That single comment changed the way I thought about donor engagement. What I had seen as inspiring transparency felt to her like exposure. It was a lesson in humility: donors may want to *see* impact, but our clients must always *feel* safe, respected, and in control of their own stories.

As nonprofit leaders, we walk a delicate line between authenticity and protection. Donors deserve to understand the impact of their investment, but never at the expense of a client's dignity. Ethical, trauma-informed fundraising requires us to ensure that every interaction, whether a tour, event, video, or story, centers the wellbeing and autonomy of the people we serve.

In the past, many organizations asked clients to share personal, emotional "tell-all" stories to move a room to tears. Today, that approach is widely recognized as harmful. It can retraumatize survivors, turn lived experience into performance, and reinforce a power dynamic where a person's worth is tied to the drama of their pain.

If a client chooses to share their story, treat them as the expert they are, not as a testimonial. Compensate them for their time and expertise. Provide coaching, preparation, and most importantly, permission to keep personal trauma private. Empower them to focus on the insights they've gained, the solutions they believe in, and the change they now help create.

Principles of Ethical and Trauma-Informed Donor Engagement

- **Dignity before visibility.** Never trade client privacy for publicity. Every tour, photo, or video should be reviewed through the lens of respect and consent.
- **Choice and control.** Give clients ownership over how, when, and whether they participate in donor-facing activities. They can always say no without repercussions.
- **Informed consent.** Explain exactly how their words, image, or story will be used and where it will appear. Ensure they understand and agree fully.
- **Safety over spectacle.** Avoid surprise visits or emotional ambushes. Prepare both donors and clients for interactions so no one feels objectified or unsafe.
- **Compensation equals respect.** Pay clients for speaking, consulting, or participating in donor events. Their expertise and vulnerability have value.
- **Focus on outcomes, not wounds.** Highlight progress, resilience, and systemic impact, not the details of individual suffering.
- **Reflect and review.** After any engagement, debrief with both clients and staff. Ask: *Did this feel empowering? Would we do anything differently next time?*

When done with care, trauma-informed engagement enhances donor connection. Donors still feel deeply moved, but through empathy grounded in dignity rather than pity. They see transformation instead of tragedy, strength instead of suffering. Ethical storytelling doesn't sanitize pain, it contextualizes it. Trauma-informed practice ensures that every story shared builds power for the person telling it, not the person hearing it. When your organization protects and honors clients this way, you model integrity.

Ethical Storytelling and Donor Engagement Checklist

Use this as a guide before any donor tour, event, interview, or story collection. This checklist is a framework for how your organization shows respect, maintains trust, and practices trauma-informed engagement in every interaction. Whether you're hosting donors onsite, preparing a client to share their experience, collecting photos, or speaking to the media, these guidelines ensure that transparency never comes at the expense of dignity. Every encounter with clients and donors is a reflection of your values.

Before Engagement

- ☐ Have we obtained clear, written informed consent from any client who may be visible or quoted?
- ☐ Has the client been told exactly how their story, image, or name will be used, and for how long?
- ☐ Have we offered compensation or an honorarium for their time and expertise?
- ☐ Have we reviewed potential risks or emotional triggers with the client and staff?
- ☐ Have we clearly explained that participation is voluntary and that they can withdraw consent at any time?

During Engagement

- ☐ Are we ensuring client comfort, privacy, and safety throughout?
- ☐ Are staff and donors briefed on trauma-informed interaction (no probing questions, no surprise introductions, no photos without consent)?
- ☐ Are we focusing conversations on outcomes, progress, and solutions—not on personal trauma details?
- ☐ Do we have a quiet space or support plan if anyone becomes overwhelmed?

After Engagement

- ☐ Have we debriefed with clients and staff to reflect on how the experience felt?
- ☐ Have we followed up with gratitude and transparency about next steps (photos, publication, media)?

- ☐ Are we using client stories respectfully in context, without exaggeration or editing that distorts meaning?
- ☐ Have we stored and shared materials securely to protect privacy?

Guiding Question

Does this engagement empower the client and uphold their dignity, or does it risk reducing them to their story?

When your organization consistently applies these checks, you create a culture where storytelling builds power, not exposure, and where donors see the kind of integrity that defines true impact.

Summary—The Fifth Factor: Partnership

Donors are the partners who help bring your vision to life once the foundation is strong. When the first four factors—Plan, Outcomes, Budget, and Team—are working in sync, the fifth factor, Donors, becomes a natural extension of that alignment. Fundraising stops being a scramble for support and becomes a shared investment in a credible, achievable future.

Partnership is the proof that your organization's internal discipline translates into external confidence. Donors fund clarity, not chaos. They look for organizations with a plan grounded in data and purpose, outcomes that demonstrate real change, a budget that proves sustainability, and a team capable of execution. When you show all four, fundraising becomes less about convincing and more about inviting.

The work of the fifth factor is to build and sustain trust. A well-qualified donor pipeline keeps the process humane by matching interest and capacity with authenticity. The annual fund and major gifts are not competing strategies but connected streams that flow from the same source: a belief in your mission. Stewardship ensures that belief endures, turning one-time givers into lifelong allies.

In the end, partnership is about transformation. When you fund the full three-year picture under one clear case, honor the people you serve, and communicate results with integrity, you close the loop between purpose and investment. This is the power of scaling with purpose, the realization that sustainability is not achieved by chasing dollars, but by aligning people, plans, and purpose around a shared vision for impact.

Key Takeaways

- **The Five Factors™ work as one system.** Donors are the natural outgrowth of a strong plan, measurable outcomes, a sustainable budget, and a capable team.

- **Fundraising is partnership, not pursuit.** When you qualify donors thoughtfully and invite them into your mission, giving becomes collaborative, not transactional.
- **Clarity builds confidence.** Presenting one comprehensive, three-year plan that integrates operations, growth, and capital gives donors proof of stability and vision.
- **Stewardship drives retention.** Consistent communication, transparency, and ethical storytelling turn early gifts into long-term relationships.
- **Donors fund readiness, not rescue.** The strongest campaigns are led by organizations that demonstrate competence, alignment, and momentum before the first ask.
- **Scaling with purpose means closing the loop.** Every plan, outcome, budget, and team decision should lead back to one goal: building trust strong enough to fuel the future.

Progress Check

After reading this chapter, rate where your organization is on a scale of one to five, with one being that your organization does not have this component, or is just beginning to work on it, and five being that your organization is fully operational and has this element ready for vetting by a major donor. Out of a maximum of 25 points, the goal is to score at least 20.

Notes:

Conclusion

Scaling with Purpose—The Five Factors™ in Action

This book was written for the nonprofit leaders who are tired of being told to "do more with less." For those who are ready to stop chasing the next grant, planning the next gala, or inventing the next buzzword, and instead build something lasting, disciplined, and transformational.

Built around Plan, Outcomes, Budget, Team, and Donors, the Five Factors™ Framework gives nonprofit leaders a coherent operating model—one that moves beyond survival mode and enables them to manage their organizations with clarity, confidence, and intention.

Each factor reinforces the others:

- **A strong plan** creates direction and alignment.
- **Clear outcomes** prove progress and earn trust.
- **A sustainable budget** turns vision into action.
- **A capable team** ensures execution and continuity.
- **Engaged donors** provide the fuel that scales impact.

When all five are in balance, fundraising stops being a crisis response and becomes the natural result of organizational readiness. Donors are being invited to invest in a mission that already works, not patch holes.

The Courage to Lead Differently

This is not a quick fix, and it's certainly not a checklist to be completed and filed away. It's a discipline, a way of leading built on honesty, courage, and accountability. Too many nonprofits have been conditioned to hide the truth: to underprice their budgets so they appear lean, to avoid measuring outcomes that might expose weaknesses, and to chase visibility instead of building true viability. The organizations that endure, the ones that truly thrive, are those willing to face reality head-on.

Courageous leadership begins with naming the real cost of your work, even when it feels uncomfortable to do so. It means being transparent

DOI: 10.4324/9781003746218-7

about what's working and what's not and understanding that vulnerability builds trust more than polished perfection ever will. It's about choosing to invest in people and the infrastructure that sustains the mission before adding more programs that stretch the organization too thin. And it means treating donors not as ATMs or paychecks but as genuine partners in the mission, people who share in the responsibility and pride of progress.

Donors don't expect flawlessness. What they value most is integrity and forward motion, a clear sense that your organization is learning, adapting, and growing with purpose. When they see that kind of authenticity, they don't just give; they invest. They join you. They stay. And together, you build something that lasts.

Revisit Your Five Factors™ Assessment

When you first opened this book, you measured where your organization stood across the Five Factors™: Plan, Outcomes, Budget, Team, and Donors. That assessment captured your starting point on the path to sustainability. Now, take time to revisit it. Gather your team and walk through each factor again. Score yourselves honestly. Reflect on what has changed and what still needs attention.

Ask:

- Where have we made the most progress?
- Which areas still need investment or clarity?
- What new insights have emerged about how these elements connect?

Keep your results. Compare them to your original scores. Use them as a roadmap for the next 12–18 months. This reassessment is not about judgment; it's about momentum. Each time you repeat it, you'll see growth that is measurable, grounded, and real.

Repeat this process annually, before strategic retreats, board planning, or budget cycles. Let it become part of your organization's rhythm of reflection and renewal. The Five Factors™ are not static; they evolve as your mission grows. Sustainability is not an outcome. It's a practice, one that begins anew each time you choose to plan with clarity, act with courage, and lead with purpose.

The Work Ahead

If you've made it to this point, you've already taken the most important step in recognizing that sustainability isn't a dream or a stroke of luck. It's a deliberate design. The next step is the real work: implementation.

Begin by gathering your leadership team and committing to move through each of the Five Factors™ together. This isn't something that can be delegated to one person or squeezed into a weekend retreat. It's a shared journey that will require coordination, honesty, and time.

Start by taking a hard look at where you are now. Use the tools and exercises in this book to audit your systems. Where are you strong? Where are the gaps? What processes need to be rebuilt, documented, or aligned? Let the answers guide your next steps.

Then, give yourself a timeline. Real change doesn't happen in a single planning session; it happens over months of consistent, thoughtful work. Plan for 12–18 months to fully integrate the Five Factors™ across your organization. Approach it as a transformation, not a project.

As you go, don't hesitate to bring in expertise when needed: a financial coach to sharpen your budget, a data analyst to refine your outcome metrics, or a facilitator to help guide difficult conversations. But remember: this process belongs to you. Consultants can support, but they can't substitute for internal ownership.

Finally, build accountability into everything. Create simple dashboards to track progress, hold regular check-ins, and celebrate milestones along the way. Internal and external transparency keeps the process alive and reinforces trust among your team and your supporters.

It will take time. It will take resources. It will take grit. But the outcome is worth every ounce of effort: a nonprofit that is stable, credible, and built to last. When done well, this work produces a culture of clarity, courage, and collaboration that can weather any challenge and propel your mission forward for years to come.

The nonprofit sector stands at a crossroads. The world doesn't need more organizations; it needs stronger ones. Those that plan boldly, measure honestly, budget realistically, empower their teams, and invite donors into partnership will define the next era of social change. When you apply the Five Factors™ with discipline and heart, you stop surviving and start scaling with purpose, because thriving isn't accidental, it's designed. And the world is waiting for what your organization can do next.

Bibliography

Chiropractic Future. Case Study: The Future of Chiropractics. (2021). *Chiropractic Future strategic plan*. https://chiropracticfuture.org/about-us/history/

BoardSource. Leading with Intent: BoardSource Index of Nonprofit Board Practices. (2021). https://leadingwithintent.org/

Oracle. (2019, August 14). "Where do donations go?" *The NonProfit Times*. https://thenonprofittimes.com/webinar/71-of-nonprofits-struggle-to-measure-outcomes-new-study-reveals-insight-hope/

Social Value UK. (2020). *A guide to social return on investment (SROI)*. Social Value UK. https://socialvalueuk.org/wp-content/uploads/2020/08/SROI-Final-Report-Assured-12Aug20.pdf

Stanford Center on Philanthropy and Civil Society (PACS). (n.d.). *Stanford Social Innovation Review (SSIR)*. Stanford University. https://pacscenter.stanford.edu/resources/ssir/

The Shelter for Abused Women and Children. (2024a). *The cost of domestic violence in Collier County*. https://naplesshelter.org/COST/

The Shelter for Abused Women and Children. (2024b). *The shelter impact report, 2023–2024*. https://www.flipsnack.com/theshelternaples/2024-the-shelter-impact-report/full-view.html

The Shelter for Abused Women and Children. (2024c). *The 2023 estimated cost of domestic violence in Collier County*. https://naplesshelter.org/wp-content/uploads/2024/05/2023-Estimated-Cost-of-Domestic-Violence-in-Collier-County.pdf

Wick, C., & Parada, A. (2020). *Estimating the local impact of intimate partner violence and the value of domestic violence programming: A study of Collier County, Florida in 2018*.

Wick, C., & Parada, A. (2020). *National assessment on the state of fundraising for domestic violence organizations*. Sharity Global. https://sharityglobal.com/case-studies/case-study-assessing-financial-stability-of-dv-shelters/

Index

For Product Safety Concerns and Information please contact our EU representative GPSR@taylorandfrancis.com
Taylor & Francis Verlag GmbH, Kaufingerstraße 24, 80331 München, Germany

www.ingramcontent.com/pod-product-compliance
Ingram Content Group UK Ltd.
Pitfield, Milton Keynes, MK11 3LW, UK
UKHW022354190926
475702UK00015B/2296
9781041253310